Join our mailing list to be notified of new products!

www.scholasticartepress.com

Copyright © 2022 by Scholastic Arte Press All rights reserved. This book or any portion thereof may not be reproduced or used in any manner whatsoever without the express written permission of the publisher except for the use of brief quotations in a book review. Printed in the United States of America First Printing, 2022 Scholastic Arte Press www.scholasticartepress.com

Table of Contents

Introduction 1

Mismatched Values: 4
   11 Relationship Red Flags You Shouldn't Ignore 4

Communication Breakdown: 9
   10 Signs of Poor Interaction Skills 9

Trust Issues: 14
   Recognizing 8 Red Flags in a Partner 14

Inconsistent Behaviors: 18
   6 Warning Signs of Unreliable Partner 18

Gaslighting Tactics: 22
   8 Red Flags of Manipulation in Relationships 22

Signs of Controlling Partner: 26
   10 Red Flags in Dating 26

7 Financial Red Flags: 31
   Money Matters in a Romantic Relationship 31

Jealousy and Possessiveness: 35
   9 Signs of Unhealthy Attachments 35

Unresolved Baggage: 40
   Recognizing 8 Red Flags from Past Relationship 40

Boundary Violation: 44

9 Red Flags of Disrespectful Behavior 44

Unrealistic Expectations: 49

8 Red Flags of Imbalance Relationship 49

Family and Friends' Opinions: 53

When Others Spot Red Flags 53

Insecurity Indicators: 57

8 Red Flags of Emotional Instability 57

Intimacy Issues: 61

6 Warning Signs of Withholding Affection 61

Lack of Empathy: 65

8 Red Flags in a Partner's Emotional Response 65

Avoiding Accountability: 69

Recognizing 8 Red Flags of Irresponsibility 69

Isolation Tactics: 74

9 Red Flags of Social Isolation in a Relationship 74

Anger and Aggression: 78

7 Warning Signs of Potentially Abusive Behavior 78

Neglecting Boundaries: 82

7 Red Flags of Disregarding Personal Space 82

Dismissive Behavior: 86

10 Red Flags of Uninterested Partners.. 86

Communication Red Flags: 90

9 Signs of Dishonesty or Evasion 90

Physical Intimacy: 94

9 Warning Signs of Discomfort and Pressure 94

Unwillingness to Compromise: 99

11 Red Flags of Rigidity 99

Red Flags in Online Dating: 104

Spotting 8 Potential Scams 104

Respecting Consent: 108

Recognizing 10 Red Flags in Intimate Situations 108

Blurred Lines: 113

8 Red Flags in Undefined Relationships 113

9 Red Flags of Commitments Issues: 117

Fear of Moving Forward 117

Respect for Time: 121

Recognizing 8 Red Flags of Chronic Lateness 121

Red Flags of Entitlement: 125

10 Signs of Self-centered Behavior 125

Future Planning: 129

9 Red Flags of Evasiveness 129

Manipulative Love: 134

8 Warning Signs of Coercive Control 134

Mismatched Life Goals: 138

9 Red Flags of Incompatible Futures 138

Red Flags of Neglect: 142

8 Signs of Unresponsive Partner 142

Blatant Disrespect: 146

Recognizing 9 Red Flags of Disregard 146

Social Media Clues: 150

Recognizing 9 Red Flags of Privacy Disregard 150

Red Flags of Flirting with Others: 154

Signs of Potential Cheating... 154

Apology Red Flags: 158

5 Signs for Differentiating Sincere from Manipulative 158

Gaslighting Signs: 162

Recognizing Red Flags of Manipulation 162

Ignoring Intuition: 166

Why Dismissing Gut Feeling is a Red Flag... 166

Red Flags of Hidden Relationship: 170

Signs of Secrecy... 170

Signs of Dismissive Behavior: 174

6 Red Flags in Communication... 174

Introduction

In the compelling exploration of relationships titled "Recognizing the psychopaths in your midst: A woman's guide to recognizing toxic relationships in the age of tinder and online dating, By: Jenna Dewan," the author delves into the intricacies of human connections, dissecting various aspects that can either nourish or jeopardize them. The book is a comprehensive guide, strategically divided into fifteen chapters, each unraveling distinct facets of relational dynamics.

The initial chapters address fundamental concerns surrounding communication and trust – essential pillars in any healthy relationship. "Communication Breakdown" adeptly exposes red flags indicative of poor interaction skills, while "Trust Issues" meticulously outlines warning signs in a partner's behavior. The narrative skillfully navigates through the realms of reliability, unveiling the subtleties of inconsistent behavior and gaslighting tactics that signify manipulation.

Financial and attachment-related red flags take center stage in the subsequent chapters. The author unveils the intricacies of money matters in romantic relationships, shedding light on the significance of financial compatibility. Simultaneously, the exploration of jealousy, possessiveness, and unresolved baggage provides readers with invaluable insights into recognizing unhealthy attachment patterns.

"Respect and Boundaries" dissect the importance of mutual respect and the potential pitfalls of boundary violations. Unrealistic expectations and the impact of family and friend opinions on relationships are thoughtfully addressed, emphasizing the role of external perspectives in spotting red flags.

Emotional stability and communication, pivotal elements in any successful partnership, are scrutinized in detail. The book meticulously identifies insecurity indicators, intimacy issues, and a lack of empathy as critical red flags that demand attention. Responsibility and accountability are further explored, with a focus on avoiding accountability, isolation tactics, and warning signs of potentially abusive behavior.

Chapters dedicated to personal space and interests highlight the significance of maintaining individuality within a relationship. Disregarding personal space, dismissive behavior, and communication red flags become crucial markers in assessing the health of a partnership. Flexibility and honesty are also examined, with an emphasis on recognizing red flags of rigidity, online dating scams, and signs of dishonesty or evasion.

The exploration extends to commitment and future plans, underscoring the importance of defined relationships and identifying commitment issues. Warning signs of entitlement, evasiveness in future planning, and the perils of coercive control take center stage, urging readers to be vigilant.

In the latter chapters, the focus shifts towards disregard and emotional unavailability, with blatant disrespect, social media clues, cheating, and manipulation under the spotlight. The author adeptly dissects the nuances of these complex issues, providing readers with the tools to navigate the intricacies of their relationships.

The book culminates with a profound discussion on trusting one's instincts and the dangers of dismissing gut feelings. Hidden relationships, secrecy, and dismissive behavior in communication are thoroughly examined, urging readers to pay heed to these red flags.

With its meticulous exploration of the intricacies of human relationships, "Recognizing the psychopaths in your midst: A woman's guide to recognizing toxic relationships in the age of tinder and online dating" serves as an indispensable guide for anyone seeking to navigate the complexities of love and connection.

Mismatched Values:
11 Relationship Red Flags You Shouldn't Ignore

Love is a journey of friendship and feelings. New and exciting relationships can turn into strong and lasting ones if you share the same values with your partner. Our values are things we believe in and care about. It makes us different from others and defines how we see the world. If two people in a relationship have different values, staying in a happy relationship usually becomes impossible. It's important to notice and discuss such problems as soon as possible, so you can have a healthy and happy relationship.

Here are some key red flags to consider:

Red Flag # 1: Scrolling Through Love: An Obsession with Social Media

In this digital age, staying connected is easier than ever, but what happens when your partner seems more engrossed in scrolling through social media than in spending quality time with you? If their attention is persistently split between you and their screen, it's worth pondering whether your values are truly in sync. Take a moment to consider if their priorities align with yours, as a healthy relationship should be built on genuine human connection rather than virtual distractions.

Red Flag # 2: The "Crazy" Ex Conundrum

We've all had our fair share of past relationships, and it's common to have a story or two to share. However, if your partner constantly labels all their exes as "crazy," it's a sign that something deeper might be at play. It could indicate a reluctance to take responsibility for their role in past dynamics, raising a critical eyebrow toward their accountability. A strong and respectful relationship involves acknowledging past connections, even if they've ended, and learning from them.

Red Flag # 3: Silent Seas: Lack of Communication

Communication is the heartbeat of any relationship, and if your partner frequently clams up during discussions about important matters or avoids open conversations altogether, it's more than just a communication glitch. It's a glaring red flag that could lead to misunderstandings, resentment, and the eventual erosion of the relationship's very foundation.

Red Flag # 4: Profile vs. Reality: A Mismatched Dating Persona

The modern tale of swiping right. So, you've swiped right and met someone who seems perfect on paper. But as you get to know them better, you realize their dating profile doesn't quite match who they really are. This misalignment can indicate a lack of authenticity and honesty, which are vital components of a strong relationship. Remember, true connections are built on genuine personalities, not digital facades.

Red Flag # 5: Chains of Control: Overly Controlling Behavior

Love should set you free, not confine you. If your partner displays controlling behavior, such as dictating your actions, isolating you from loved ones, or surveilling your every move, it's time to hoist the red flag. Healthy relationships thrive on trust and autonomy, and controlling behavior can make you suffocate.

Red Flag # 6: Lies Weave a Web: Frequent Lying

Honesty is the cornerstone of a healthy relationship. If your partner keeps telling lies, whether they're small or big, it's like a warning sign and indicates that being truthful and trustworthy might not be one of their values. A relationship that's built on lies is like a house made of cards that can fall at any time.

Red Flag # 7: Green-Eyed Monster: Controlling or Jealous Behavior

A little jealousy from time to time is normal, but when it seems like your partner is trying to control all of your actions is a Big Red Flag! A healthy relationship is built on the basis of mutual respect and trust, and if these two elements are lacking, then it is time to reconsider the values in your relationship. If your partner gets super jealous and controls you all the time, it could mean that they don't value your freedom and individuality, which are really important for a good relationship.

Red Flag # 8: Lost in Translation: They Don't Listen to You

Feeling unheard or dismissed can be incredibly frustrating. If your partner ignores you or acts like they don't care when you talk, it's a sign that they might not respect your thoughts and feelings. A strong relationship needs both people to listen and talk openly, so watch out if this keeps happening.

Red Flag # 9: Words Can Sting: Constant Put-Downs

Playful teasing is one thing, but constant put-downs and belittling comments will badly affect your mental health. If your partner repeatedly makes hurtful remarks or undermines your self-confidence, it's time to reevaluate the values at play. These hurtful remarks can damage the emotional well-being of both individuals in a relationship. Healthy relationships should uplift and empower each other, and not the other way around.

Red Flag # 10: Mirror, Mirror: Feeling Low Self-Esteem

Your partner should be your biggest cheerleader, not the cause of your self-doubt. Low self-esteem might lead to a pattern of seeking constant validation, feeling excessively jealous or insecure, and being overly dependent on the partner for a sense of identity. Ignoring this warning sign could eventually lead to a toxic dynamic, hindering both individuals' growth and happiness. It's important to address and support each other's self-esteem struggles openly, fostering an environment of understanding, empathy, and encouragement to nurture a healthy and thriving relationship.

Red Flag # 11: The Narcissism Warning

Relationships thrive on empathy, compromise, and mutual care. You know, those times when someone's all about themselves, constantly needing admiration, and just can't seem to show genuine empathy for others? Yes, that's a major sign. If you start noticing this kind of behavior in your partner, it's not something to brush aside. So, trust your gut and don't ignore those red flags – they're there for a reason!

In conclusion, recognizing and addressing mismatched values is vital for the health and longevity of any relationship. While differences are natural, ignoring red flags can lead to resentment, frustration, and eventual breakdown. Remember, a harmonious relationship isn't about erasing differences, but about embracing them while working together to create a beautiful symphony of shared values and understanding.

Communication Breakdown:
10 Signs of Poor Interaction Skills

Talking to each other can build or break how we get along. It's really important for relationships, but if we don't talk well, we might not know where we stand with each other. Talking is super important in our lives. It helps us share our thoughts, wishes, and emotions, and also get what others are saying. In this section, we'll explore ten red flags that indicate poor interaction skills and offer insights into improving them.

Sign # 1. Avoiding Eye Contact

Maintaining eye contact is a basic yet crucial aspect of effective communication. When we talk to others, looking into their eyes shows we're paying attention and interested. If someone avoids looking you in the eye during a conversation, it might signal discomfort, lack of confidence, or disinterest. It can make the other person feel like you are not interested, even if you are. Eye contact helps us connect and understand each other better. So, remember, looking into someone's eyes is like showing them you're listening and you care. It's an important part of talking and getting along with people, it shows that you are attentive and engaged in the conversation.

Sign # 2. Rambling or Interrupting

Talking too much without letting others speak or interrupting them during a chat can show that you're not very good at talking and listening. Good communication involves active listening, allowing others to express their thoughts before sharing your own. It can make the other person feel ignored or annoyed, and they might not want to talk with you again. Good talking means taking turns and really listening to what the other person is saying. Respectful pauses contribute to a smooth conversation flow. So, next time you chat, try not to talk too much and let others share their thoughts too.

Sign # 3. Ignoring Nonverbal Cues

Nonverbal cues like facial expressions, gestures, and body language play a significant role in communication. When we talk, our faces and bodies tell secrets without words. Ignoring these hints is like not listening with our eyes. Failing to notice or respond to these cues can lead to misunderstandings. Good talks need eyes and ears, not just words. So, pay attention to the quiet messages hiding in how people move and look. It helps us truly connect and have better chats.

Sign # 4. Overusing Jargon

Using too many complicated words and phrases that others don't understand is like talking in a secret code. It can make people confused and feel left out. Good communication is like a bridge that connects us, and overusing jargon can weaken that bridge. It's important to use words that everyone can understand so that everyone can be part of the conversation. When we keep it simple and clear, we're showing that we care about making sure everyone is on the same page. So, remember, less jargon, more understanding!

Sign # 5. Lack of Empathy

Empathy involves understanding and sharing another person's feelings. When people don't show care about how others feel, it's a clue that their talking skills might not be so good. This "lack of empathy" means they don't understand or share the emotions of the person they're talking to. This can make the talk feel one-sided and not friendly. Displaying empathy fosters a supportive environment and enhances communication. Good talking requires us to listen and care about others. When we have empathy, we make the other person feel important and heard.

Sign # 6. Failure to Summarize

Not summarizing or paraphrasing what the other person has said indicates a lack of active listening. You need to say back stuff to check if you got it right. Like nodding your head when someone talks. If you don't do this, it's like you're not really listening. Summarizing helps clarify your understanding and demonstrates that you value the other person's input. It also provides an opportunity for correction if there's a misunderstanding. Good talks need this, so you both know what's what.

Sign # 7. Negative Body Language

Crossed arms, fidgeting, or standing with a closed-off posture can convey defensiveness or a lack of interest. It's like talking without words, and it can show you're not interested or open. Positive body language, such as maintaining an open stance and nodding, encourages a positive atmosphere and encourages open dialogue. If we don't use positive body language, people might think we're not friendly or don't care about what they're saying.

Sign # 8. Poor Time Management

Constantly arriving late, rushing through conversations, or monopolizing someone's time can undermine effective communication. When we don't respect others' time or talk too much, it can lead to problems. Respecting others' time and being mindful of the duration of your interactions promotes healthy communication dynamics. Good chats need balance and patience, and valuing time is part of that. So, if you find it hard to manage time during talks, it's a hint to work on your interaction skills.

Sign # 9. Using Excessive Filler Words

Excessive use of filler words like "um," "uh," or "like" can make you appear unsure or unprepared. It can make you seem unsure or not ready to talk. Minimizing the use of these fillers helps you convey your thoughts more confidently and coherently. So, next time you talk, try to, you know, avoid using too many of those extra words. It will help you talk more clearly and show that you're confident when you speak.

Sign # 10. Inadequate Feedback

Providing constructive feedback is a vital aspect of effective communication. If you shy away from sharing your thoughts or avoid addressing issues, it can lead to unresolved conflicts. Offering feedback in a respectful and solution-oriented manner contributes to better understanding and collaboration.

In a world where communication is a fundamental tool for connecting with others, poor interaction skills can hinder personal and professional growth. By recognizing these ten red flags and making a conscious effort to improve our communication skills, we can build stronger relationships, enhance collaboration, and navigate challenges more effectively.

Trust Issues:
Recognizing 8 Red Flags in a Partner

Trusting someone with your emotions and life might take some time, but there comes a time when it becomes a sacred part of your bond. However, if you think they are hiding something from you, or not telling you the truth, it's time to realize your partner has serious trust issues.

So, here are some signs that someone might have trouble trusting, which can help you see the red flags in your partner.

Sign # 1 Always Expecting the Worst from You

Have you noticed that your partner often seems to expect you to let them down, even when you've never given them a reason to think that way? This could be a sign of trust issues. Even kind gestures and compliments might be met with skepticism, as they struggle to believe in your sincerity. Healthy relationships thrive on recognizing each other's strengths, but when trust is absent, the focus tends to shift toward the flaws. So, if your partner frequently assumes the worst and seems fixated on your shortcomings rather than your strengths, it could very well be a red flag of underlying trust issues.

Sign # 2 The Secretive Shell

Everybody has their personal boundaries, which is completely okay. However, if your partner has built a wall around their life that raises doubts about their intentions or character, it could indicate that something isn't quite right. Trust is built on honesty and openness, much like the foundation of a strong house. But when someone purposely keeps important aspects of their life hidden or avoids sharing their thoughts and actions, it raises questions about what's being concealed and why. Even if they long for meaningful connections, someone grappling with trust issues might struggle to let people get close or be hesitant to reveal their true selves.

Sign # 3 You Guys Don't Share Mutual Respect

One of the primary indicators that your relationship is suffering is a lack of respect. Respect is the foundation of any healthy relationship, and when it begins to wane, it can indicate that something is wrong. Mutual respect involves treating each other well and valuing each other's feelings and boundaries. So, when there's a lack of mutual respect, it can suggest that there are underlying issues with trust between the people involved.

Sign # 4 Blaming without Reason

When people trust each other, they give them the benefit of the doubt. It means they believe the other person is good and wouldn't do something bad without a proper reason. But when someone starts blaming you without a valid explanation, it shows they might not trust you like they used to. Blaming without reason can be a sign that the trust between people is shaky. When trust weakens, it's like the strong bridge between them gets weaker too. To keep that bridge strong, it's important to communicate and understand each other before assuming the worst and blaming without a good reason.

Sign # 5 Commitment Issues

Trust is like a strong foundation in a relationship or any situation. If someone has trouble committing, it might mean they are worried about getting hurt, disappointed, or let down. This worry usually comes from not having enough trust in the other person or the situation. So, commitment issues can be a sign that someone needs more trust to feel secure and confident about making promises or sticking with something. Just like a house needs a solid foundation to stand tall, commitment needs trust to stand strong.

Sign # 6 Unwilling to Admit the Responsibility

Unwillingness to admit responsibility for one's actions can be a sign that someone is having trouble trusting others. When people find it hard to accept that they did something wrong, it might be because they fear being judged or criticized. Trust involves feeling safe and comfortable with others, knowing that they won't be treated harshly or unfairly. If someone lacks trust, they might avoid admitting their mistakes because they worry about negative consequences. It's like they're protecting themselves from potential harm by not being open about their actions. So, difficulty in admitting responsibility can indicate a deeper issue of not fully trusting the people around them.

Sign # 7 They are Overprotective

When someone is overprotective, it means they might feel like they need to control everything around them to feel safe. They might be afraid that if they don't watch closely or try to manage everything, something bad might happen. This can happen because they find it hard to believe that things will be okay on their own. So, being overprotective is like a way of showing that they have a hard time trusting that things will work out well without their constant attention. It's like their trust in the world is a bit shaky, and they want to hold onto it tightly.

Sign # 8 They are Snooping around your Private Life

Invading someone else's private life is never a positive sign. When someone begins checking your social media or looking at your phone without telling you, it indicates that they are concerned about who you're talking to. This strongly hints that there's not much trust between you two. As an illustration, they might ask lots of questions if something different occurs like if you come home later than usual, they could want to know all the details.

Remember, trust issues don't mean someone is a bad person. It just means they've had some tough experiences that make it hard for them to believe in others. If you notice these signs, try to talk with your partner kindly and understand what they're feeling. Trust is something that can grow over time with patience and care.

Inconsistent Behaviors:
6 Warning Signs of Unreliable Partner

Trust and commitment in a relationship are shown when someone acts the same way consistently. Inconsistent people can be nice and close one moment, but distant or unavailable at other times. This confuses and upsets the other person. It's odd to see people act differently in relationships. Couples can't feel safe in their love if there's no consistency. When you're in a relationship, you should always be able to count on your partner, no matter what. It's like having a reliable beat in a song that keeps everything in harmony, even when things get tough.

Given how important consistency is in a relationship, it's surprising how many people end up in a relationship with an inconsistent partner and put up with it. Regardless of the cause, here are 6 red signals to be aware of.

Sign # 1: Lack of efforts

The relationship may appear to be one-sided. You are working hard, making time for your partner, and attempting to be emotionally transparent with them. However, no matter what you do, they do not reciprocate. Instead, it feels like you're grinding your teeth to get them to see you or respond to your texts. In turn, they do the bare minimum to keep you interested. This is known as breadcrumbing. The breadcrumbs do everything they can to keep their partner eager for attention, keeping them chilly until they decide that someone better has arrived. Lack of effort can lead to feelings of unappreciation and neglect, which can damage your self-esteem over time.

Sign # 2: Unpredictable behavior

Your worst relationship will be with a person who sends confusing signals all the time. They continually make you wonder where you fit in their world. You'll never feel completely at ease with them because it's difficult to know what they're thinking. Because they are unpredictable, it's natural to be concerned that they will wake up one day and decide the relationship is finished. They keep you at a distance when you need to know them the most. It's difficult to be optimistic about the relationship's endurance because they're so difficult to interpret.

Sign # 3: Their words don't match their actions

In a relationship, consistency is when a partner shows their feelings to back up their statements. Consistent partners, on the other hand, guarantee that their behavior matches what they're talking to you, so there are no questions. When a relationship transitions from the honeymoon phase to a level of comfortability, words might get stale in the inconsistent relationship.

A partner who says, "I love you," yet treats you as a burden. They refer to you as their companion, but they refuse to open up to you, rely on you in times of need, or be there for you when you need them. They claim to want to spend more time with you, but they are constantly busy, and you rarely see or hear from them. They make lofty promises but lack a specific plan or any true potential to keep them. They only tell you what you want to hear. However, as good as their words sound, the inevitable mismatch between their words and actions, as well as their lack of follow-through, just leaves you disillusioned and progressively frustrated.

Sign # 4: Breaking Promises

The inability to keep promises or follow through on commitments is one of the most visible indications of inconsistency. Individuals that are inconsistent may make promises but fail to keep them, resulting in disappointment and a loss of confidence. Consistency is a love language that demonstrates dependability and reliability. When a partner makes promises, their mate can be confident that they will be kept. A constant partner is concerned about how the other person perceives them. Breaking promises will only disappoint a significant other, which is the last thing a reliable person wants to do. The ultimate priority is to be the one person on whom the other person can rely.

Sign # 5: Being Indecisive

Being indecisive is a warning sign of an unreliable partner because it shows a lack of commitment and clarity. When someone is unable to make decisions or constantly changes their mind, it creates uncertainty in the relationship. An unreliable partner might struggle to follow through on their promises or commitments, leaving their significant other feeling unsure about their intentions.

Indecisiveness can lead to frustration and confusion for both partners. It can make it difficult to plan for the future or make important decisions as a couple. Additionally, an indecisive partner may struggle to provide the emotional support and stability that a relationship requires.

Sign # 6: They Don't Respect your time

Not respecting your time is a clear warning sign of an unreliable partner. When your partner consistently disregards or wastes your time, it shows a lack of consideration and commitment. An unreliable partner may frequently cancel plans, arrive late, or fail to prioritize spending quality time with you. This behavior can lead to frustration, disappointment, and a sense of being undervalued in the relationship. It indicates that your partner may not take your feelings or the relationship seriously, and this can erode trust and emotional connection over time. In a healthy and reliable partnership, both individuals respect and honor each other's time, demonstrating their commitment and dedication to building a strong bond.

It can be difficult to understand relationships, especially when things appear hazy or confusing. You may save time and energy on a relationship that might not work out by being aware of the warning indications that someone might not want to be in a relationship with you. Remember that everyone has diverse intents, therefore these indications should not be taken as absolutes. Trust your instincts, be open with each other, and put your own pleasure first. You ought to be with someone who values your relationship and envisions a future together.

Gaslighting Tactics:
8 Red Flags of Manipulation in Relationships

When your partner is manipulating you, they exploit you in an excellent way to impact your choices and influence your life. Gaslighting is one sneaky way manipulators use to gain more control. They do this by making you doubt yourself and your beliefs. Slowly, gaslighting chips away at your self-confidence, leaving you unsure of yourself. Gaslighting isn't picky; it can affect anyone and is a go-to move for those who want power. In this section, we will explore eight red flags that could indicate gaslighting in a relationship, helping you recognize and address these harmful behaviors.

Sign # 1. Discrediting Your Memory

A common gaslighting tactic is to question your memory of events, leaving you feeling unsure about your memory. When your partner is always challenging your memory, this might be a sign that something's not right for you. Statements like "You're overreacting, that didn't happen that way" can make you doubt yourself and that's why trusting your memory is important. Remember, your experiences are yours and it's okay to trust your memory and stand your ground when your experiences are questioned. Healthy relationships respect your thoughts and feelings.

Sign # 2. Withholding Information

People who manipulate might hide information or change the story on purpose to control what's happening. They might make their actions seem less important or leave out important details to make you doubt yourself. If you see that what they're saying doesn't match up, it's really important to ask them and find out what's true. They're hiding things to make you see things their way. But you shouldn't just ignore your doubts. Good relationships need honesty and trust. If something doesn't feel right, it's okay to talk about it. Your feelings are important.

Sign # 3. Fake promises

Some folks can make things sound super amazing, even when they're not. Don't fall for their fancy words. Instead, watch out for what they're really up to. They might promise you something great, but when it's time to deliver, they don't follow through. It's like they're hiding important stuff until you agree, and this is all to keep you from seeing what they're really up to (which is trying to control you more). So, be careful and don't believe everything you hear. It's better to be cautious and not let them take advantage of you.

Sign # 4. Shifting Blame

Pointing fingers at others is a major signal of gaslighting in relationships. When someone avoids taking responsibility for their actions and starts pinning the blame on you, it's a big red flag. They might say things like, "You made me do this" or "If you didn't act that way, I wouldn't have reacted like that." This manipulation messes with your head, making you doubt yourself and your role in things. Healthy relationships are all about sharing the blame when needed and owning up to mistakes. If you notice this blame-shifting pattern, it's time to stand tall and recognize you deserve better than this.

Sign # 5. Isolation from Support Systems

A person trying to isolate you and make it harder for you to leave them is someone who tries to turn your network of support against you. Gaslighters might try to isolate you from friends and family who could offer an outside perspective. These people whisper things that make you doubt your family or closed ones, making you feel like they're not on your side. This confusion ends up bringing you back to the gaslighter, exactly where they want you. They could discourage your interactions or make you feel guilty for seeking advice. But keep in mind that maintaining connections with supportive people is crucial to help you see the situation clearly.

Sign # 6. Playing Victim All the Time

They act like they're always getting hurt, making you feel guilty and confused. They're good at making you believe you're the one causing all the pain in the relationship. Trust your gut and question the situation. Healthy relationships are a two-way street, with both sides taking responsibility. So, if you're feeling like the bad guy all the time, it's time to step back, see the bigger picture, and don't let anyone toy with your emotions.

Sign # 7. Creating Confusion

Gaslighters often create confusion by contradicting themselves or denying things they previously said. They say one thing today, another tomorrow, leaving you feeling like reality is slipping through your fingers. They play memory games, making you question if you're the forgetful one. For example, the same person that's criticizing you and making you feel worthless suddenly starts praising you for something you've done. This makes you feel even more unsettled. You might start thinking, "Maybe they're not that bad after all." But remember, they are still the same. This tactic can make you question reality and your ability to comprehend situations accurately. Keeping a record of conversations can help you keep track of these inconsistencies.

Sign # 8. Twisting Reality

Ever met someone who's a reality bender? Manipulators may twist reality by distorting facts or using selective memory. They twist reality like a pretzel, leaving you questioning what's real and what's not. They might deny their own saying or doing hurtful things, causing you to doubt your own perception. When they use this reality-twisting trick, it leaves you feeling lost, not knowing who to believe. So always trust in your experiences and don't let anyone undermine your sense of reality as a gaslighter never stops lying.

Gaslighting is a harmful manipulation technique that can erode your self-confidence and mental well-being. Recognizing the red flags is the first step toward protecting yourself from such toxic behavior. If you notice these signs in your relationship, it's essential to address them openly and set boundaries. Remember, you deserve respect, understanding, and a relationship built on trust. If manipulation continues, seeking support from friends, family, or professionals can help you navigate the situation and prioritize your emotional health.

Signs of Controlling Partner:
10 Red Flags in Dating

The feeling of being protected by your partner is amicable, but it's essential to keep an eye out for signs that might indicate they are controlling you. Trust, respect, and open communication are the foundations of a healthy relationship, and when someone else is defining the rules of your life, it's time to wake up. In this article, we'll explore 10 red flags that could suggest you're in a controlling relationship.

Sign # 1. Criticism — Even for Small Things:

Healthy partners encourage and support each other's growth. If your partner constantly criticizes you, especially for minor matters, it might be a sign of control. Constructive feedback is one thing, but constant negativity can erode your self-esteem. Criticism, when cloaked in the guise of caring, can be tricky to spot. Your partner might say, "I only want what's best for you" or "I'm just trying to help you improve." While improvement is a natural part of any relationship, it should be a joint effort, with both partners learning and growing together. If the "help" feels more like a directive, it's time to take a closer look.

Sign # 2. Making Decisions for You:

A controlling partner might make decisions for you without considering your feelings or opinions. It's essential to have a say in matters that affect your life, and decisions should be a collaborative effort. In a healthy relationship, both people have an equal right to make decisions. It's like teamwork – you both bring your thoughts and ideas to the table. When one person starts making all the decisions, it can make the other feel like their thoughts don't matter.

Sign # 3. Inability to Accept Criticism:

A balanced relationship involves both giving and receiving feedback. If your partner can't handle any criticism or becomes defensive and hostile when you express your thoughts, it could indicate a controlling nature. If they can't accept criticism, they might be more focused on keeping a tight grip on the relationship. By avoiding criticism, they could be avoiding a loss of control. This behavior can lead to a cycle of misunderstandings and tensions. By nurturing open communication and seeking solutions, you can work together to break down barriers and create a stronger, healthier bond.

Sign # 4. Frequent Jealous Accusations:

Trust is vital in any relationship. If your partner is often jealous and accuses you of wrongdoing without evidence, it might signify their insecurity and desire to control your actions. Jealousy-driven accusations can lead to isolation. If your partner is constantly doubting your loyalty, they might discourage you from spending time with friends and family, making you more dependent on them for social interaction. If you find yourself trapped in a cycle of accusations and control, don't hesitate to seek help and explore ways to improve your relationship dynamics.

Sign # 5. Constant Monitoring:

Healthy relationships allow for personal space and independence. If your partner constantly monitors your activities, checks your messages, or insists on knowing your whereabouts at all times, it's a potential red flag. When one partner constantly monitors the other, it indicates a lack of trust and confidence. Trusting your partner means believing in their intentions and respecting their ability to make their own choices. It's important to foster open communication, trust, and the establishment of healthy boundaries to ensure that both individuals can grow and thrive together.

Sign # 6. Conditional Acceptance, Caring, and Attraction:

Love should be unconditional and based on genuine affection. If your partner uses affection, caring, or attraction as bargaining chips or manipulates you by threatening to withdraw them, it could indicate a controlling dynamic. In a healthy relationship, love should flow freely, unburdened by conditions. You might believe that your partner's concern is a reward that can be taken away if they are not controlling. Healthy love is about supporting each other's growth and happiness without ulterior motives

Sign # 7. Gaslighting:

The goal of gaslighting is to cause you to doubt your own perceptions by distorting or denying reality. A controlling partner might use gaslighting to undermine your self-confidence and maintain control over the relationship. Gaslighters may shift blame onto you for things that aren't even your fault. They might make you feel guilty or ashamed for things you shouldn't. You deserve to be in a relationship where your worth and emotions are respected.

Sign # 8. Sabotaging Your Progress:

Healthy relationships are built on mutual support and encouragement. A controlling partner may downplay the importance of your goals or discourage you from pursuing them. They might prioritize their needs and aspirations over yours, leaving you feeling unimportant. If your partner intentionally hinders your personal or professional growth, it's a sign that they are trying to maintain power over you.

Sign # 9. Questioning Your Reality:

Controlling partners may manipulate situations or twist conversations to make you doubt your understanding of events. Controlling partners sometimes play mind games, making you doubt your memories and perceptions. They might twist things around to confuse you, making it hard to trust yourself. If you frequently question your memory or judgment, it's worth examining the dynamics of your relationship. Trusting your instincts and seeking an outside perspective can help you regain your sense of self and make informed decisions about your relationship.

Sign # 10. Disregarding Your Opinion:

In a healthy relationship, both partners' opinions and viewpoints should be respected. If your partner frequently criticizes your ideas, it can be a sign that they want to dominate and control you. The force that binds relationships is open and honest communication. When your opinions are brushed aside, it can create a communication breakdown, leading to frustration and misunderstanding.

For a relationship to be strong and balanced, it's important to recognize the warning signals of a dominating partner. Setting limits, being transparent with your relationship, and putting your needs first are all important. Consider asking for help from friends, family, or a therapist if you spot multiple of these warning signs in your relationship so that you can address the problems and protect your happiness and mental well-being. Keep in mind that a truly loving relationship is one in which both individuals encourage and nurture one another.

7 Financial Red Flags:
Money Matters in a Romantic Relationship

Discussing finances with your partner can be tricky, especially if you're unsure about their thoughts or lack knowledge about managing money. People have different views on earning, spending, and investing money. Unfortunately, conflict about money and finances can lead to deeper marital concerns, such as so-called financial perjury, in which people hide their spending from their partners.

Look at these 7 financial red flags; if any of these seems familiar, it's time to take action!

Sign #1: Avoiding Money Discussions

It's difficult to discuss finances with a loving partner. Putting your spending habits, debt, credit score, and financial objectives on the table can feel awkward and vulnerable, especially if you aren't precisely where you want to be financially. And you are not alone in those emotions. In fact, according to a recent survey, individuals would rather talk about mental illness, drug addiction, politics, race, and religion but not money. Isn't it strange? However, there is a significant difference between feeling uncomfortable when discussing money and simply refusing to engage in the subject. A partner who refuses to discuss money could be doing so for a number of reasons, all of which are cause for concern.

Sign # 2: Hidden Debt Dilemmas

Debt is a part of life for many, but hidden or excessive debt can strain a relationship. If your significant other isn't truthful about owing money or makes light of the amount they owe, it's a warning sign, especially if you're thinking about getting married later on. This is concerning because you might end up sharing that burden. Both the owed money and the dishonesty are problems in this situation. It's not advisable to immediately break off the relationship just because they have debt. Instead, it's important to carefully think about how you'll navigate the relationship once you're aware of this. A key thing to think about is how your partner handles repaying debt - are they taking initiative or avoiding the issue? If they are motivated to pay off the debt then it's not a sign to be worried about but if it's the opposite then you know the answer.

Sign # 3: Dishonesty Regarding Finances

Individuals experiencing a lack of control over their finances often keep parts of their money matters secret. This secretive behavior about money can harm your relationship. It involves not being honest about money owed, earnings, and undisclosed spending and accounts. Imagine discovering a receipt for a big expense they made, and when you mention it, they react defensively. Normally, this wouldn't bother you, but if you're both saving money for something you both want to do later, this purchase will reduce your savings. If your partner is caught and still lies about it, that's a serious warning sign!

Sign # 4: Mysterious Money Moves

Consider it a potential concern if your partner's money habits don't seem to make sense. Money matters connect with mental well-being and how we handle spending. If spending is always hard to control, it could indicate deeper issues. Giving too much, buying things you know they can't afford, or lending too much to friends and family are all signs. Avoiding going out or refusing to spend money can also raise concerns. Excessive spending beyond your means can strain the relationship. Pushing for extravagant purchases or pressuring your partner into spending more than they're comfortable with is not healthy. It's important to respect each other's financial limits and goals.

Sign # 5: Failure to Repay Borrowed Funds

Giving money to your partner might feel normal in a relationship, as helping each other is common. But pay attention to how your partner handles money. If you've lent money before, you understand it can be tough to get it back, especially if it's your loved one. It's even worse if your partner doesn't stick to their promises and you have to keep asking for your money, only getting excuses. That's a warning sign; you should consider stepping away from the situation!

Sign # 6: Seeking Approval for Financial Choices

If your partner comes from a family where everyone shares money, it's possible that making financial choices together might be restricted. Having separate bank accounts or sharing accounts with partners might not be encouraged. This means even small money decisions might need approval. While advice and family discussions are okay, they shouldn't stop you from making your own money choices. Phrases like "I need to ask my parents" or "My family handles these things" can be a warning sign. While it might seem like this mostly affects men, it's not a good look for anyone to always seek permission for money decisions.

Sign # 7: Using Money to Manipulate or Shame

Forcing someone to pay for things because they have more money is not right. Equity in the financial contribution is important. If one partner is consistently contributing significantly more or less than the other, it can lead to feelings of resentment or imbalance. Nobody is perfect with money, so it's good to talk about it nicely. But making someone doubt their own thoughts is not okay. Using money to control or make someone feel bad is a warning sign in a relationship. It's not a healthy way to treat each other. Money should be about fairness and understanding, not about power or making someone feel small. If someone uses money to manipulate or shame, it's important to talk about it and find a better way to communicate and share expenses.

In conclusion, a healthy relationship is built on trust, communication, and shared values - and this extends to your financial matters. If you notice any of these financial red flags in your relationship, it's crucial to address them openly and honestly. Remember, addressing these issues early can prevent them from growing into larger problems. By working together, you can create a solid and secure financial future for both you and your partner.

Jealousy and Possessiveness:
9 Signs of Unhealthy Attachments

Attachments are like strong ties that connect two people, bringing them close emotionally, mentally, and spiritually. It's like a special cord that links them together. Healthy attachments are built on trust and open expression of feelings. Every attachment has a bit of jealousy and possessiveness, and each person is worried about losing and sharing their loved ones. But when jealousy and possessiveness become too much, it can lead to unhealthy attachments, making the other person feel suffocated.

Let's look at 9 major signs of unhealthy attachments that everyone should be aware of before getting close to someone. These signs can also help individuals strengthen themselves if they're going through a difficult attachment.

Sign # 1: Constant Phone Monitoring

Frequently snooping through your partner's phone and pressuring them for access to their social media accounts is a sign of possessiveness and insecurity. It indicates a lack of trust within the relationship. In healthy connections, trust forms the foundation. However, the overwhelming presence of jealousy can stifle the very essence of a relationship, corroding its vitality and giving rise to emotional unrest. It's essential to acknowledge that a genuine relationship flourishes when both individuals share mutual freedom and honor each other's boundaries, eliminating the need for nosy surveillance.

Sign # 2: Endless Suspicion

Trust is the cornerstone of any relationship, be it a close friendship or a romantic bond. Unrelenting doubt signals a lack of faith in your partner. In good relationships, trust is the main thing, and people don't usually think negatively about each other. If someone is overly jealous or controlling, it can create doubts and make it hard to build a strong bond based on trust. Having too many doubts can ruin a relationship and make it hard to be happy together.

Sign # 3: Excessive Rules and Regulations

Too many strict rules and constant commands show that someone is being overly jealous and controlling. This happens because they don't trust the other person and want to control everything they do. Good relationships are built on trust and giving each other space. But if there are too many strict rules, it stops the person from growing and feeling free. In a healthy relationship, trust and giving space help both people grow. But if there are too many rules, it's a sign of an unhealthy attachment.

Sign # 4: Turning Achievements into Pain

When accomplishments that should bring joy start causing pain, it could be linked to jealousy and possessiveness within a relationship. When a partner feels envious, they might downplay your achievements or make them about themselves. This can lead to feelings of hurt and confusion. Likewise, possessiveness can make your successes a point of contention, as if they belong to your partner. A healthy relationship celebrates each other's triumphs.

Open communication is key. Address the emotions behind the pain and work together to build trust and support. True partnership thrives on shared happiness, not on turning accomplishments into sources of anguish.

Sign # 5: Emotional Unavailability

The cardinal rule of all attachments is to never let your loved one feel alone, particularly when you're together. In good relationships, it's important to give each other comfort when your partner is feeling down. But in relationships where one person is too controlling or jealous, it's hard to find that comfort. Partners who are toxic can make things worse by not showing affection and avoiding connecting emotionally. This can create a big gap between you and them, making it feel like they're not there for you. Sometimes, they even lie to cover up their mistakes.

Sign # 6: Lack of Emotional Availability

When someone is too jealous and possessive in a relationship, they might not be there for you emotionally. Excessive jealousy and possessiveness can lead to emotional neglect. Partners who exhibit these traits may disregard your feelings and fail to offer support when needed. This emotional unavailability translates to a lack of empathy during moments of sadness or stress. If your partner's jealousy and possessiveness hinder their ability to provide care during your difficult times, it might signify an unhealthy relationship unsuited for your well-being.

Sign #7: Bad Temper

Getting really angry all the time can make people wonder what you're really feeling in a relationship. If your partner often can't control anger, it might mean they are actually feeling pretty jealous and wanting to control things a lot. In a good relationship, trust and understanding help keep emotions in check. If you notice signs of jealousy and wanting to control things when your partner gets mad, talking about it can make your relationship stronger and more peaceful.

Sign #8: Keeping a constant eye on every move

Watching someone all the time, like always checking their phone or getting involved in everything they do, shows too much jealousy and possessiveness. This means not trusting them enough and wanting too much control. This behavior isn't good for a strong relationship. It might make the other person feel trapped and not able to be themselves. In a good relationship, there's trust and space for each person.

Sign #9: Love Trials

Subjecting your partner to love tests, such as incessantly checking their messages and becoming upset over their interactions with others, unveils shades of jealousy and possessiveness. These emotions could be red flags for an unhealthy attachment. In genuine affection, trust and independence hold sway. If you or your partner feel compelled to regulate or constantly monitor each other, it's a potential sign of a shaky foundation. Wholesome love is built on understanding, encouragement, and mutual respect. Should you identify these signs, it's advisable to have an honest dialogue with your partner or seek guidance to ensure your relationship remains resilient and joyful.

Recognizing and addressing signs of jealousy and possessiveness is vital for nurturing a healthy and thriving relationship. Open communication, trust, and respect for each other's individuality are key to breaking free from these negative patterns. Remember, a strong bond is built on love, support, and the freedom to grow both as individuals and as a couple.

Unresolved Baggage:
Recognizing 8 Red Flags from Past Relationship

When we dive into new relationships, it's essential to navigate our emotions with caution. Sometimes, we carry along unresolved baggage from our past relationships, which can cast a shadow on our current bond. Just like an expert in relationships, we must learn to recognize the red flags that signal trouble ahead. In this section, we'll explore how to spot these warning signs and ensure smooth sailing in your romantic journey.

Red Flag # 1. Trust Your Gut Feeling:

Have you ever had a feeling deep inside, like a whisper from your heart? That feeling guides you through life's twists and turns and that same feeling tells you that If something doesn't feel right, don't just ignore it. Your gut feeling can help you sense when something doesn't match up. Maybe your new partner says one thing but does another. Often, our subconscious mind picks up on cues we might miss consciously. If your gut feeling is sending off warning signals, take a step back and evaluate the situation.

Red Flag # 2. Communication Patterns:

Effective communication is the anchor of any healthy relationship. Observe how your partner communicates with you and others. Do they listen actively, or do they dominate conversations? Are they respectful and considerate of your feelings? If they often interrupt, don't listen, or seem controlling, these could be signs of problems they haven't resolved before. Past baggage can lead to communication issues, so pay attention to how your partner expresses themselves.

Red Flag # 3. Consistency Matters:

Consistency is the shining star in any relationship. If your partner's behavior fluctuates dramatically, it might be a sign of unresolved issues. For example, if they shower you with affection one day and then become distant the next, it could indicate deeper emotional struggles. When someone's consistent, it shows they're sincere and true. But if someone's behavior keeps changing, it might mean they're struggling with something inside, perhaps from a past relationship. Consistency helps us learn from our past experiences. If you notice the same patterns of behavior that caused problems in previous relationships, it's a clear warning sign.

Red Flag # 4. Recognizing Behavior Patterns:

Patterns from past relationships can seep into new ones if not addressed. Are you noticing familiar dynamics, like feelings of inadequacy or power imbalances in your new relationship too? These could be warning signs of unresolved baggage resurfacing. By spotting these behavior pieces, you might start to notice if someone is acting in ways that remind you of a not-so-great relationship you had before. When you pay attention to these patterns, you can decide if they're healthy or if they're like warning signs that you should be careful.

Red Flag # 5. Emotional Baggage Impact:

Understanding how emotions from before can influence how we see problems in past relationships is really important. Unresolved emotional baggage can impact self-esteem and mental well-being. If your partner shows signs of extreme mood swings, unwarranted jealousy, or persistent negativity, it's crucial to address these issues early on. Being aware of this can help us separate our past feelings from what's happening in the present. So, paying attention to how we feel and recognizing if those feelings are connected to the past can really help us see warning signs in our new relationships.

Red Flag # 6. Reliability and Commitment:

A sturdy relationship requires trust and commitment. Be cautious of repeated excuses or unfulfilled commitments. When you keep your promises, it shows you care and are serious about the relationship. If your partner struggles to do the same, it could be a sign that they're dealing with problems from their past that are affecting how they act now. Being committed means you're willing to work through problems together. If your partner avoids talking about issues or runs away from tough situations, it could mean they're carrying emotional baggage from before.

Red Flag # 7. Self-Awareness and Growth:

Healthy relationships thrive on self-awareness and personal growth. If your partner seems unwilling to reflect on their past experiences and learn from them, it could be a sign that unresolved baggage is clouding their judgment. By connecting the dots, we become better at making choices. We might choose to talk with our partner about it or decide it's best to move on. Either way, we're making a choice that's good for us. So, understanding ourselves and growing stronger is like having a special tool to spot signs from our past relationships.

Red Flag # 8. Emotional Distance:

Emotional distance is when you feel like there's a barrier between you and your partner. It's like an unsaid feeling that something isn't quite right. By paying attention to this feeling, you can uncover hints of past issues sneaking into the present. Difficulty expressing emotions or maintaining emotional intimacy could result from past relationships where vulnerability was met with hurt or rejection. When someone is emotionally distant, they might not give you the time and attention you need. They might seem distant or preoccupied like their mind is somewhere else. If you struggle to open up to your current partner, unresolved emotional baggage may be influencing your behavior. By paying attention to how you and your partner feel, communicate, and connect, you can uncover these clues and create a smoother journey ahead.

As we embark on new romantic journeys, it's vital to recognize the red flags that may arise from unresolved baggage. Trust your intuition, pay attention to communication patterns, and be vigilant about consistency and commitment. By identifying these warning signs early on, you can navigate around potential obstacles and create a healthier, more fulfilling relationship. Remember, just keep learning from the waves of the past, you too can learn to steer clear of turbulent waters and get started on your journey toward a smoother relationship.

Boundary Violation:
9 Red Flags of Disrespectful Behavior

Respecting boundaries in a relationship is not merely a courtesy but a fundamental pillar of nurturing a healthy and thriving partnership. Boundaries can be described as invisible lines that define individual preferences, needs, and restrictions. By mutually following these boundaries, you create an environment where both partners can feel secure, understood, and valued. Have a look at 8 boundary violation red flags to help you navigate tricky Disrespectful Behavior.

Red Flag # 1. Invading your Personal Space

When someone persistently enters your personal space without your consent, it is one of the first indications of disrespect. If you find someone repeatedly standing too close, touching you without consent, or invading your personal conversations, it's a clear indication that they may be crossing the line. This can make you feel uncomfortable and disrespected. If you notice this behavior, it's important to communicate your discomfort politely and assertively. Respecting personal space is a fundamental aspect of showing consideration for others.

Red Flag # 2. Disregarding Your Feelings

Another red flag is when someone constantly dismisses your feelings or opinions. In a respectful relationship, constructive feedback is valuable, but consistent criticism that disregards your feelings and devalues your opinions is a warning sign. Healthy communication involves showing empathy and understanding, even when offering suggestions for improvement. If you find yourself in a situation where your feelings are consistently undermined, it's essential to address the issue and reaffirm your need for respect.

Red Flag # 3. Exploit you

Negative behaviors like manipulation and exploitation can damage your sense of control and self-worth. Beware of people who try to control your behavior or emotions by making you feel guilty, using emotional blackmail, or using gaslighting. These strategies are designed to undermine your confidence and lead you to give in to their demands, frequently at the expense of your own well-being.

Red Flag # 4. Ignoring Consent and Preferences

Respecting consent is paramount in any interaction. If someone repeatedly dismisses your decisions or disregards your preferences, they are violating your boundaries. This could display in various ways, such as pressuring you into activities you're not comfortable with or refusing to accept your refusal. Always remember that you have the right to set limits and expect them to be honored. It's crucial to establish firm boundaries and stand your ground when someone tries to breach them.

Red Flag # 5. Crossing Communication Boundaries

In any relationship, effective communication is essential. It's disrespectful when someone constantly ignores your efforts to communicate, talks over you, or interrupts you. Meaningful conversations involve active listening and an exchange of ideas. If someone consistently monopolizes the conversation or belittles your contributions, it's a clear indication that they may not be valuing your voice.

Red Flag # 6. Overstepping Emotional Boundaries

Boundaries also apply to emotions and sensitive topics. A persistent attempt to get you to divulge personal information or offensive remarks about your emotions are examples of emotional boundary violations. You are entitled to control when and how you express your feelings. Informing the other person that you feel uncomfortable talking about certain topics is completely acceptable. Healthy relationships involve mutual respect for each other's emotional limits.

Red Flag # 7. Got a problem with your availability and activities

Respecting someone's time and availability is another crucial aspect of maintaining boundaries. Disrespectful behavior becomes evident when someone constantly interrupts your activities or disregards your schedule. This could be through making frequent calls, sending messages, or showing up unexpectedly when they are aware of your commitments. Everybody has the right to choose how to spend their free time. To stop further boundary violations, it's critical to address the issue if someone consistently disregards this matter.

Red Flag # 8. Undermining Personal Choices

Respecting individual choices is fundamental in any relationship. If someone consistently questions or undermines your decisions, it could indicate a lack of respect for your autonomy. While constructive feedback can be helpful, constant criticism or attempts to manipulate your choices can be damaging. Keep in mind that others should respect your decisions because they are yours to make.

Red Flag # 9. Overstepping Digital Boundaries

In today's digital age, our online presence plays a significant role in our lives. However, even in the virtual world, boundaries matter. It's a clear boundary violation when someone repeatedly invades your digital space by reading your private messages or disclosing your personal information without your permission. The rules of respect are not modified just because it is online. Watch who has access to your digital life carefully, and make sure your boundaries are respected.

Our emotional health and the caliber of our relationships depend on us being able to maintain healthy boundaries. To promote a more respectful and peaceful environment, it's critical to recognize these subtly offensive behaviors. Here is what you should do if you encounter these red flags:

- **Communicate:** Express your feelings and concerns with the person involved. Honest communication can help them understand your boundaries and the impact of their behavior.

- **Set Limits:** Clearly define your boundaries and let others know what is acceptable and what is not. Be assertive in maintaining these boundaries.

- **Seek Support:** If the behavior continues despite your efforts, consider seeking support from friends, family, or professionals who can offer guidance and assistance.

- **Prioritize Self-Care:** Taking care of your emotional well-being is crucial. Engage in activities that bring you joy, practice mindfulness, and surround yourself with people who respect and value you.

Respectful behavior must be identified and rectified if healthy relationships and personal well-being are to be maintained. It's crucial to assertively communicate your boundaries and expectations if you experience any of the warning signs listed above. If the behavior persists, you might need to think about restricting or ending your contact with the person in order to safeguard yourself from emotional harm. Always keep in mind that you deserve to be treated with respect and kindness. To ensure that your interactions are always respectful and enriching, take the time to recognize these warning signs and take proactive measures to address them.

Unrealistic Expectations:
8 Red Flags of Imbalance Relationship

Many couples experience unreasonable expectations during their romantic journey, leading to disappointments. These expectations can stem from various sources, such as societal influences, media portrayals, or personal experiences. When we set unrealistic expectations, we create a vision of how our relationship should be that might not align with reality. It can result in unattainable standards, disagreements, resentment, a breakdown in communication, dissatisfaction, and detachment. It can make one partner feel their needs aren't satisfied, which may lead to distrust and anger. Let's review 8 red flags indicating an imbalance in relationships.

Sign # 1: Expecting your partner to always agree with you

Although the idea of constantly agreeing with your partner may seem appealing, it is impractical to expect this to happen. Each of you has your own distinct ideas, viewpoints, and opinions because you and your partner are two separate individuals. In addition to being unavoidable, disagreements can also lead to personal development and mutual understanding. The important thing is not to agree on everything, but rather on how these differences are handled with open discussion, mindful listening, respect for one another, and constructive compromise.

Just keep in mind that having different perspectives gives your relationship integrity and strength.

Sign # 2: Expecting your relationship to be romantic every time

This one can be blamed on rom-coms, social media, and advertising.

Everywhere we look, we see great romantic gestures and love energy between fictional characters, as well as between couples on social media and people on billboards.

For the greatest impact, everything is turned up to the highest setting, which gives us the impression that what we already have is inadequate. In reality, the newly engaged couple posting from the Bahamas also argues about things like leaving socks lying around the home. If they don't fight about it in the beginning, you can be sure they will a few years down the road.

According to a study, persons who frequently post about their spouses have low self-esteem and are looking for external validation. So perhaps it's not that amazing, after all.

Sign # 3: Expecting your partner to not be friends with the opposite gender

You and your girlfriend have only been dating for a few weeks or months, but you're already preoccupied with the number of male acquaintances she has. You've either asked her to unfriend all her male friends so that you're the only MAN in her social circle, or the other way around, depending on how things have gotten to this stage. You're doing it completely wrong then.

My friend, trust must be developed in relationships for them to be successful, not try to be hidden from others.

Sign # 5: Expecting your partner to read your mind

It is unrealistic to expect your partner to continuously understand your thoughts and feelings, and doing so may cause them to fall into the risky habit of overthinking everything. Instead, give context by discussing your feelings and how you saw the event to help lead more fruitful dialogues. When this expectation develops, think about whether a talk about showing more consideration for one another can address a deeper need for connection and support.

Sign # 6: Expecting your partner to always say the right thing

Even in movies, we can see that communication isn't always perfect. Just like in real life, people can make mistakes when they talk. Your partner isn't always going to say things perfectly because they're human, just like you and me. It's not fair to expect them to always get it right. In a relationship, it's not healthy to treat your partner like they're there just for your amusement. They're not always going to say the exact right thing, and that's okay. We all make mistakes sometimes, even when we don't mean to. Remember, your partner is a person with feelings and emotions, just like you. It's important to understand that everyone messes up and says things they didn't mean to. As long as they weren't trying to hurt your feelings on purpose, it's okay to forgive them.

Sign # 7: Expecting Your partner to be the Source of all of your happiness

People frequently start relying on their relationships to fulfill all of their needs. This comprises objectives, success-oriented drive, amusement, and even happiness. It is impossible to be happy in this entangled connection when you begin to base your happiness on anything other than yourself, let alone your partner. It is advised that you make an effort to create and cultivate your own future plans. Consider the activities that you enjoy doing on a personal level.

Sign # 8: Expecting everyone in your life to like your partner

It is absolutely normal for the people around you to not like your partner as much as you wish they would. After all, it will be you who spends most of your time with your partner. It is just impossible to expect everyone you know to love the person you love because everyone has the freedom to like or dislike someone. We all have distinct thoughts about what a person ought to be like. This explains why our responses to the same person vary over time. Your partner will feel secret pressure to behave in a specific way in order to be loved and make you happy if you expect everyone in your life to like them. That is unquestionably an awful way to start a relationship. While attempting to strengthen some of your partner's positive traits so they can do better in society, be prepared to accept other people's preferences.

We all have expectations, but a relationship doesn't have to be destroyed by them. Come together as partners and express your expectations. Keep the conversation going. You could require professional assistance if one of you is hesitant to make sacrifices or maintains unreasonably high expectations. You can get through the difficult parts with the help of a counselor who genuinely wants to see your relationship prosper.

Family and Friends' Opinions:
When Others Spot Red Flags

The advice provided by our family and friends can prove incredibly valuable in navigating various kinds of relationships, be it romantic, professional, or friendships. These are the people who are closest to us, who support us, and who are concerned about our interests and happiness. They sometimes exhibit the ability to spot details that we might miss in the heat of the moment, such as relationship red flags. Let's examine why it's crucial to pay attention when others raise these warning signs and how doing so will ultimately help us in the future.

1. The Power of Outside Perspective

Consider yourself going through a dense forest. Since your attention is on the path in front of you, you can miss potential dangers or pitfalls. It can be similar in relationships since sometimes our feelings and hopes make us blind to forthcoming issues. The outside viewpoint of our family and friends is crucial at this point. They may provide a new, objective perspective that enables us to perceive details we might have otherwise overlooked. Having a close-knit group of loved ones is wonderful since they have a different perspective on us. They are very familiar with our routines, responses, and dreams. They are able to detect oddities and suspicious situations because of their personal understanding they are able to connect dots that we would not perceive because of their outsider perspective, which makes their analysis extremely significant.

2. The Genuineness of Concern

Our loved ones sincerely love us. They only care about what is best for us and have no ulterior motives. They frequently want to shield us from potential danger, which is why they raise concerns or identify warning signs. Even though it may occasionally be challenging to accept their opinions, it is imperative to keep in mind that their motivations are based on love and concern.

3. Recognizing Patterns

It can be challenging to spot patterns in our own life at times, especially when we're in the thick of things. Friends and relatives can spot patterns that could point to more serious problems since they have more of an opinion. Although we might not be able to see these patterns, they could be red flags of something more serious. By paying attention to their observations, we make it easier for us to spot these trends and take proactive measures to deal with them.

4. The Value of a Reality Check

It's simple to miss potential red flags during the joy of daily life or the excitement of a new relationship. We can get a much-needed reality check from our loved ones. They are not deceived by the initial burst of feelings; rather, they are based on a deeper comprehension of ourselves and the dynamics at work. We can examine the problem more objectively and come to wise judgments with the help of their opinions.

5. The Importance of Trust

Any connection, whether it be with a partner, friend, or family member, is built on trust. We acknowledge the depth of our relationship with our loved ones when we put our trust in their judgment. We're stating that we respect their viewpoints and have faith in the power of our relationship. Trusting their assessment of warning signs does not imply that we are giving up control of our lives; rather, it means that we are using their knowledge to help us make better decisions.

6. Honesty and Open Communication

Maintaining open communication is crucial when our loved ones express worries. We're given a chance to learn more about the problem through these discussions, which will help us make better decisions. We may share our feelings and experiences in a secure environment when there is an honest and open conversation. Red flags are simpler to spot when we're encouraged to express our worries, anxieties, or doubts in an open manner. We can share any discomfort we may be experiencing in this setting, and our friends and family can assist us in determining whether such sensations are a sign of possible issues.

7. Growth Through Shared Wisdom

The interactions we have with individuals who are close to us can offer us great chances for personal development. By carefully weighing their points of view, we hone our intuition and make better decisions. Our personal growth journey is enhanced by accepting the knowledge of our loved ones. The emotional support of friends and family is priceless during difficult circumstances. They offer a secure environment where we can express our challenges, anxieties, and aspirations. In return, they provide understanding, support, and helpful guidance. In addition to assisting us in navigating difficult situations, this emotional support also promotes emotional development and resilience. Our general well-being can change significantly when we realize we're not alone in this.

In the end, it is important to Balance Independence in your personal growth

While family and friends perspectives are important, it's important to strike a balance between them and our own independence. We must have faith in our ability to make choices that are consistent with our beliefs and goals since, in the end, we are the ones living our lives. Respecting the opinions of our loved ones does not imply giving up our freedom; on the contrary, it enhances our decision-making.

The views of our family and friends are very important in the tangled situations of life. They serve as our reliable pillars of support, mirrors that reflect truths we may not otherwise perceive, and lighthouses that guide us through storms. When others notice red flags, it's not a condemnation of our decisions; rather, it's a monument to how well our relationships have held up. We can have healthier, happier relationships and a more rewarding life in general by paying attention to their worries, taking into account their opinions, and thoroughly considering their advice. Therefore, let's treasure these perceptions, accept the love and care that led to them, and employ them as tools to negotiate the occasionally difficult terrain of relationships.

Insecurity Indicators:
8 Red Flags of Emotional Instability

Experiencing self-doubt can adversely affect the emotional intimacy with your partner and give rise to significant challenges. Our minds are perpetually active, and certain thoughts might carry an element of uncertainty. This uncertainty can destroy your confidence, which in turn can disrupt your relationships and life. Recognizing the importance of emotional instability holds significance as it enables a deeper self-awareness and healthy relationships with people around you.

In this section, we'll talk about a few simple signs that can help us see if your partner might be emotionally unstable. We can then do things to make ourselves feel better mentally.

Sign #1: Always Being Jealous

When one person in a relationship feels like they're not as good as the other and is scared of losing them, it shows that there's a problem with feeling safe in the relationship. If they often think that other people are better than them and get upset when those people do well, it could mean that they don't feel good about themselves. When we don't feel confident in our own abilities or think we're not valuable, we tend to keep comparing ourselves to others. When this happens, jealousy is a usual reaction and it's a clear sign that your partner doesn't feel happy in the relationship. But these bad feelings can become less if they focus on getting better themselves and feeling good about who they are.

Sign #2: They have Trust Issues

Love and trust are without a doubt essential elements of a loving relationship. If your fears keep you from trusting your partner, it will be difficult to express your feelings to them. This will have a significant effect on your relationship since it will restrict the amount of emotional intimacy you may have. In general, it degrades the strength of your relationship. If you genuinely fear that you won't be able to trust your partner, you shouldn't be together. If you have love insecurity, is it even worth it? Trust is the foundation of any strong connection.

Sign # 3: They need Constant Reassurance

An insecure partner may require their partner's support, communication, and affirmation all the time. This behavior usually shows up in people with an anxious attachment style, who are always looking for affirmation of their value and their partner's affection for them out of fear of breaking up with them. In contrast, individuals with an avoidant attachment style may become emotionally distant or refrain from intimacy as a coping mechanism when they feel uneasy. While the occasional feeling of insecurity is normal, if it persists and has a detrimental effect on the relationship, it may be a sign of a disorder known as relational OCD (ROCD).

Sign# 4: They Ask a lot of Questions

An insecure partner seeks to find out as much as they can about their partner's activities, relationships, and whereabouts. If your significant other frequently asks you a lot of questions after you've merely been away for a short period of time, take that as a sign that they are battling deep-seated fears. The uncertainty they feel about themselves is reflected in these feelings, which may have nothing to do with you but permeate their daily confrontations. Unfortunately, this conduct could also indicate a controlling partner.

Sign Number 5: They don't Respect your Privacy

If your partner doesn't respect your privacy, it means they do things like going through your stuff without asking, checking your phone or social media without your permission, or always asking where you are and what you're doing. This can happen when someone feels unsure about the relationship and wants to ease their own worries. But it's not good because it can make you feel like they don't trust you and they're crossing your personal boundaries.

Sign # 6: They don't like to be left alone

For them, being by themselves is really scary if their relationship makes them feel unsure about themselves. They'd prefer to be anywhere else than left alone with their thoughts. They might decide to stay in a bad relationship that isn't good for them because they're afraid of being alone. It would be a good idea for them to talk to a counselor or share their feelings with a friend or family member who can help them see things in a new way. They could learn that it's better to be alone and focus on loving themselves, instead of staying in a harmful relationship.

Sign # 7: They Avoiding Conflict

Partners who feel unsure about themselves often try to avoid arguments in a relationship. They're scared that if they talk about what they want, what's bothering them, or if they disagree, it might make their partner very angry or even break up with them. This fear comes from their inner feelings of not being good enough or thinking they don't deserve love and care. These feelings make them really scared of having disagreements. So, instead of risking a fight, they choose to keep their thoughts and feelings inside. But this can lead to problems because not talking openly can make the relationship weaker over time. It becomes harder to deal with issues and build a strong, lasting relationship based on respecting and trusting each other.

Sign # 8: They are Apologizing too much

Does your partner think you're upset with them just because you didn't use an exclamation mark in your "Hi"? A clear sign of insecurity in a relationship is when they always think you're angry and keep saying sorry for small things. Someone who feels unsure about their relationship might be afraid of making the other person upset and leaving. For example, if someone says, "I know my girlfriend cares about me, but I still feel unsure," they might then say, "I'm sorry for feeling this way. I hope you're not mad."

The first step in fostering emotional well-being is recognizing these warning signs of emotional instability. Kindness and self-compassion must be used to resolve these issues. On this path to emotional stability, getting support from friends, family, or experts like therapists or counselors can be quite helpful. It's normal to ask for help, and being proactive about addressing these signs can result in a happier, more self-assured, and emotionally secure life.

Intimacy Issues:
6 Warning Signs of Withholding Affection

Sometimes an unexpressed discomfort regarding emotional closeness can limit an individual's capacity to establish and uphold deep relationships. This reluctance might not lead to a conscious rejection of affection from others but might introduce tension into the relationship, possibly causing it to end prematurely before a deeper emotional bond can develop.

Challenges with intimacy can be grouped into several fundamental categories, like intellectual, sexual, spiritual, emotional, or experiential hurdles.

These are some of the intimacy-related signs that your partner might be withholding affection. If you notice any of the following signs in your relationship, it could be worthwhile to take notice and act wisely upon it.

Sign # 1: Perfectionism

People who have a fear of intimacy could have a strong need to be perfect. They may feel unworthy of an enduring, meaningful relationship or love, and as a result, they strive to be flawless in order to "earn" that love. They frequently experience anxiety or insecurity when approaching others because they believe that if they are honest with people, they will be rejected or hurt. They may seek perfection in an effort to insulate themselves from this dread as it would make them believe that people would accept them more readily. This issue can be resolved by making your partner love themselves the way they are.

Sign # 2: Communication Breakdown

If you don't know what is going on in your partner's mind, there will be an awkward vibe when you both share a space like you both will be there but something won't feel right. We occasionally experience a minor glitch in our communication with our partner. You know, that might be the reason why we occasionally feel distant from one another. Talk to each other every day, even if it's just for a moment, and pay closer attention when you notice that communication is starting to break down. It may require some effort and time, but it will be worthwhile. Just like anything worthwhile, you know?

Sign # 3: You're there in body, but not in spirit

People with intimacy issues might find it difficult to be mentally present in relationships or social interactions due to past experiences or fears. You can live in the same house and still struggle with intimacy. Eye contact, avoiding technology, and being present for your partner are all simple nonverbal strategies to increase intimacy. Physical touch, like a real hug when you arrive home from work or a morning cuddle, can be very effective. These intimate gestures let the other person know they are important to you.

Sign # 4: Low self-esteem

Individuals grappling with challenges related to intimacy often find themselves locked in a struggle with their own self-worth. Forming deep and meaningful connections with others becomes a formidable task for them, entangled in a web of past wounds, the fear of rejection, and a lingering doubt in the intentions of others. This internal battle can push those with fragile self-esteem to believe they possess an inherent flaw or are undeserving of the warmth and fondness that love brings. Consequently, they might find themselves withdrawing from social interactions, inadvertently exacerbating their emotional turmoil. The absence of these vital human bonds further propels their self-esteem on a downward spiral.

The silver lining, however, lies in the fact that there exist strategies to confront and alleviate these emotional burdens. Seeking solace in the company of understanding friends, embarking on a journey of self-discovery, or even seeking professional guidance, if necessary, can all catalyze a transformative process. As they gradually recognize their own intrinsic value and cultivate faith in the authenticity of their friendships, the tides of self-esteem can remarkably shift, paving the way for profound and enriching interpersonal connections.

Sign # 5: Too much stress

You might notice that the closeness in your relationship isn't as strong since you have been experiencing stress. It might be brought on by your hectic schedule, your anxiety, or the numerous demands of your job. No matter what is happening around you, controlling your stress is crucial. A sincere conversation with a close friend or a family member you can trust is a good approach. You can be who you really are around those people. They might help you with some of your tasks if you're overburdened, and they can give you a fresh viewpoint on a challenge you're facing. You must rely on someone from your friends or family if they're willing to help you.

Sign # 6: You're married to your job

Being a workaholic is not a badge of honor; rather, it could be a serious indicator of problems with affection. Even worse, working excessive hours might harm your physical health. We may unintentionally avoid intimacy when we lose ourselves in hectic work. Lots of people tend to steer clear of getting too close to others because they want to dodge those not-so-pleasant emotions such as feeling down, burdened, or super angry. One nifty trick is to just stay occupied all the time and sidestep dealing with those icky feelings. If you've been with your partner for a while, it's easy to fall into a routine and evade intimate moments.

There are numerous indicators of intimacy issues, potential contributing factors in a relationship, and solutions for each of these. If talking to your partner doesn't work out, the best solution is to speak with a therapist. You can increase your intimacy, but you'll need to give your relationship some extra energy that may not have been present before. Start a weekly date night, but switch off each week who decides what to do. It helps you to discuss your intimate interests. Psychologists also advise spending time together at home performing activities like cooking or nurturing gardens. Talking about your likes and dislikes and posing questions to one another while engaging in these activities might also be helpful. There is a good chance that you and your partner can mend fences if you are both willing to do so.

Lack of Empathy:
8 Red Flags in a Partner's Emotional Response

Empathy is the ability to comprehend and experience another person's feelings. It is a necessary component for strong and fulfilling relationships. When your significant other shows empathy, it's like having a true supporter by your side. They uplift you, bring solace during tough times, and partake in your happiness. Moreover, they sincerely apologize if they've caused you pain and hold themselves accountable for their acts.

But what if your partner is not compassionate? Wondering how to figure out if someone isn't really connecting with your emotions and needs? So, like, watch out for these ten signs that your special someone might not be all that empathetic:

1. They're not exactly tuned in when you talk.

Do you ever notice if your words truly resonate with your partner? Are they engaged in your conversations, asking thoughtful questions, or providing meaningful input? When you open up to your partner and sense that your words fall on deaf ears, it might be indicative of a disconnect in understanding or an absence of genuine concern for your emotions. When communication feels one-sided, it's possible your partner isn't making an earnest attempt to grasp your perspective. The absence of attentive listening or apparent disinterest during these moments could imply a shortfall in the empathetic connection needed to truly comprehend your feelings.

2. They don't validate your feelings.

Emotional validation entails acknowledging and accepting how you're feeling without passing judgment. When emotions are expressed, both partners in a happy and empathetic relationship listen and demonstrate understanding. The words they might use involve "I understand why you're feeling this way" and "Your feelings are important to me." This honest and considerate response fosters connection and trust. But you know, if your partner keeps on downplaying or brushing off your emotions all the time, it might be like a hint that they don't really get where you're coming from, you know?

3. They avoid taking responsibility for their actions.

When your significant other avoids owning up to their actions, it raises a major concern that they might struggle with understanding and sharing your feelings. This conduct highlights the difficulty in acknowledging the impact of their actions on both emotions and overall harmony. In a healthy, empathetic relationship, when one partner realizes they've caused harm, they exhibit comprehension and take accountability for their behavior. This reflects a strong emotional connection. Conversely, if your partner repeatedly evades responsibility, opting to assign blame or contest their actions, it hints at a lack of genuine regard for your emotions.

4. They don't support your goals and dreams.

Empathy is all about really getting each other, feeling the same vibes, and having common dreams. It's like when your partner is totally on board with your plans and cheers you on, you know they're in sync with your emotions. On the flip side, if they're not there backing your goals, it might point to a bigger gap in how well they're tuned in to your emotions and inner wishes. It's like they might not be fully catching onto your feelings and aspirations, which are major parts of a super caring and understanding relationship.

5. They don't show appreciation or gratitude.

Understanding someone else's feelings and experiences, and expressing gratitude, go hand in hand. Sometimes, if your partner doesn't quite get this empathy thing, they might unintentionally misinterpret what you mean when you do something or fail to understand how their own behavior affects your emotions. Although it doesn't necessarily imply that they are being insensitive on purpose, it does make you wonder if they are actually aware of your feelings and capable of reacting appropriately.

6. They don't compromise or negotiate.

During those times when you and your significant other have differing viewpoints, do they make an effort to come to a mutual understanding? If your partner consistently avoids finding a middle ground or engaging in discussions, it could potentially hint at them being more invested in their own thoughts and wishes, possibly overlooking yours. If your partner shows reluctance to yield or participate in a productive conversation, it might point to a possible imbalance in how you both contribute or collaborate. When the acts of compromise and negotiation become an ongoing rarity, it might signal the importance of delving deeper into your partner's ability to empathize and their dedication to comprehending and respecting your feelings.

7. They don't respect your boundaries.

A little heads-up that your significant other could be having a hard time connecting with your feelings if they seem to brush them off or not really pay attention to the limits you've set for yourself. People who show empathy make a real try at getting where you're coming from and showing respect for those lines you've drawn. They get that people come with all sorts of different needs and likes, and they honestly want you to feel secure and treasured. So, if you're picking up on a pattern where your partner is consistently not giving weight to your boundaries, it's something worth tuning into. It might be a hint that there's a bit of a shortage of empathy lurking underneath in the relationship.

8. They don't change or grow.

When your partner consistently doesn't seem interested in growing personally, it might indicate they're overlooking how important it is to work on themselves, both for their own path and for the people around them. This could potentially give rise to worries about their capacity to understand, as it could suggest they don't fully realize the potential impact of what they say, do, and how they behave on you and the connection you have.

If you begin noticing these indications in your relationship, it might be a good thought to take a step back and rethink your relationship. Holding onto frustrations, becoming annoyed, experiencing solitude, and generally feeling low can all arise from your partner seemingly not truly grasping and sharing your emotions. You should definitely aim to be with someone who can empathize with your feelings and provide you with affection and concern.

Avoiding Accountability:
Recognizing 8 Red Flags of Irresponsibility

In a world where accountability seems to be slipping through the cracks, it's crucial to recognize the red flags of irresponsibility that often go unnoticed. From flimsy commitments to a lack of feedback, these signs can indicate a troubling trend. In this section, we'll delve into some common behaviors that might indicate someone is avoiding accountability, and more importantly, we'll explore healthier alternatives to foster a more responsible approach.

Red Flag 1: Shying Away from Goal Setting

You're in a relationship, and your partner seems to be just going with the flow without a clear direction. Setting goals? Nah, not their thing. Avoiding accountability often starts with the reluctance to set achievable objectives. It's like driving without a map – you'll end up somewhere, but it might not be where you wanted to go.

Instead: Embrace goal-setting as your compass. Establish some clear, attainable goals, and then divide them up into manageable chores. This gives you a sense of direction and ensures that you are in charge of moving forward.

Red Flag 2: Tossing the Blame Game

We've all played the blame game at some point, right? Pointing fingers and dodging responsibility is a definitive sign of evading accountability. Whether it's blaming others, circumstances, or even the weather, it's a surefire way to sidestep ownership of your actions.

Instead: Step up and own your mistakes. Accept that slip-ups happen, and rather than dwelling on blame, focus on learning from the experience and finding solutions.

Red Flag 3: Apologies? Not Their Thing

Ever encountered someone who simply can't muster up a genuine apology? Remember to keep an eye out for any more signals that can cause you to become a little concerned. It's very obvious they've made a mistake but they still appear to be having a little trouble admitting it.

Instead: When you make a mistake apologize sincerely when you're in the wrong. It's a powerful way to acknowledge your actions and mend relationships. Remember, a heartfelt apology can go a long way in building trust and respect.

Red Flag 4: The Veil of Non-Transparency

In any kind of relationship, be it personal or work-related, honesty plays a crucial role. Yet, if you notice either you or your companion keeping things back, skirting important talks, or not freely talking about what you're up to, it's a clear indicator that you might be slipping into the realm of being less accountable.

Instead: Foster open and transparent relationships by sharing your thoughts, decisions, and progress with those around you. Communication is the bridge that connects accountability and trust.

Red Flag 5. Fickling Commitments

In a fast-paced digital age, it's easy to get carried away with promises and commitments. However, a clear indicator of avoiding accountability is making commitments without proper consideration. If someone is constantly saying one thing and doing another, it's time to take notice.

Instead: Pause and reflect before making any commitments. Consider your own capacity and resources. It's okay to say no or negotiate if you're unsure about fulfilling a promise. When you do commit, ensure it's a well-thought-out decision, setting the stage for responsible action.

Red Flag 6. Neglecting Feedback

Ah, the sweet sound of silence – well, not when it comes to avoiding accountability. Irresponsible behavior often involves shutting out different perspectives. Remember, growth comes from healthy criticism and open conversations. Embrace feedback like you'd embrace your favorite comfort food after a long day.

Instead: Welcome feedback as an advantage, not as criticism. Actively seek input from colleagues, friends, or partners. Constructive feedback is a catalyst for growth and improvement. Embrace it as an opportunity to enhance your performance and demonstrate accountability.

Red Flag 7. Not Considering Your Partner's Perspective

We've all been taught to walk a mile in someone else's shoes and for good reason. Irresponsible actions often stem from a narrow viewpoint, failing to acknowledge the ripple effects on others. Time to take a step back and get a wider view. When you try on someone else's perspective, you build a stronger connection.

Instead: Practice active listening and empathy. Put yourself in your partner's shoes and consider how your choices may affect them. Cultivating empathy not only strengthens your accountability but also fosters deeper connections with those around you.

Red Flag 8. They do Overcommitment:

"Overcommit" – a classic fable of biting off more than you can chew. While multitasking might seem like a superhero skill, it often ends in more mess than success. Juggling too many responsibilities can lead to subpar results and, ultimately, the blame game. Focus on what you can genuinely manage, and give your tasks the attention they deserve. Quality over quantity should be your guiding principle.

Instead: Prioritize tasks and commitments realistically. Assess your bandwidth and allocate your time accordingly. It's better to excel in a few areas than to spread yourself thin. By managing your commitments, you showcase your responsibility and ensure your actions align with your words.

As we wrap up this enlightening discussion, remember that recognizing red flags of irresponsibility isn't about pointing fingers. It's about understanding our own behaviors and making positive changes. Whether we're talking about our connections with others or the things we do for a living, embracing our human side – quirks and all – can actually be a lifesaver when it comes to owning up to our actions. So, how about we aim for being real, stay open to different perspectives, and truly put in the effort to become better versions of ourselves? Until next time, stay accountable and keep those red flags at bay!

Isolation Tactics:
9 Red Flags of Social Isolation in a Relationship

It's really important to find the right balance between showing love and maintaining your identity in a relationship. We all know how important it is to spend time with your significant other. You are always tempted to do all of the things together - you want to eat together, watch Netflix together, and have fun together but as crucial as it may seem it is very important to have some of your personal space that only belongs to you. Having a safe personal space is very important as it acts as a home when you are feeling frustrated. In this section, we'll look at some warning signs that your relationship might be getting out of control.

Sign #1: A Hunger for Constant One-on-One Time

A relationship flourishes when both partners relish their time together and independently. However, a potential warning sign arises when one partner insists on monopolizing every waking moment. While it's natural to enjoy each other's company, feeling pressured to be in their presence 24/7 might suggest an underlying issue. Wholesome relationships encourage personal growth and exploration, so it's essential to strike a balance between togetherness and individual pursuits. You can do this by talking to your partner and letting him know about the things by which you start feeling uncomfortable.

Sign #2: The Burden of Hiding Your True Self

In a loving partnership, authenticity should be celebrated, not suppressed. It's necessary to take a step back if you find yourself keeping certain facets of your personality or interests a secret from your partner. An open line of communication and tolerance for one another's eccentricities are necessary components of a solid relationship. A partner who genuinely cares will embrace your uniqueness, fostering an environment where both of you can be your true selves.

Sign #3: Drowning in a Sea of Pessimism

A healthy relationship contributes positively to your emotional well-being. When one partner becomes a constant source of negativity, consistently belittling your dreams or undermining your self-esteem, it's a significant red flag. Partners should uplift and support each other, helping each other navigate life's challenges with a positive attitude.

Sign #4: Stuck in a Relationship Void of Affection

Intimacy and affection are the cornerstones of a fulfilling relationship. However, if your once-affectionate partner has turned distant and cold, it's time to reevaluate the situation. Feeling trapped in a loveless partnership can lead to emotional distress and hinder your personal growth. A strong partnership thrives on mutual love, respect, and the willingness to nurture each other's emotional needs.

Sign #5: Demanding Unwarranted Access

Trust forms the foundation of any healthy relationship. It can be a show of control rather than genuine care when your partner demands on knowing all of your passwords. Mutual respect for one another's independence and privacy is the foundation of all successful relationships. I know at some point when you will think that you love your partner more than anything, you will be thinking what's the big deal in knowing my social apps password but remember some things are your things and after some time you will be feeling suffocated by the constant surveillance. While it's important to share and communicate openly, the need to safeguard personal boundaries is equally vital.

Sign #6: Refusing to Engage with Friends and Family

Human connections extend beyond the confines of a romantic partnership. If your significant other repeatedly shy away from interacting with your friends and family, it could signal a deeper issue. Healthy relationships thrive when both partners respect and engage with each other's social circles, enriching each other's lives through diverse connections.

Sign #7: Excessive Codependency

Ah, codependency – the term itself might ring a bell, but what does it really mean? It's when a relationship takes a turn from being two individual souls walking side by side to becoming an inseparable duo, where personal boundaries blur and the sense of self gets lost in the mix. It's important to recognize the signs of codependency: excessive reliance on one another, feelings of worth tied solely to the relationship, and a fading sense of personal identity.

Sign #8: When Intimacy Fizzles Out

Remember those early days of butterflies in your stomach and endless conversations that stretched into the night? Intimacy was abundant, and every touch sent shivers down your spine. But what happens when that once-vibrant connection starts to fade? The intimacy may dwindle due to various reasons like busy schedules, unspoken expectations, or even a growing emotional distance. It's crucial to spot this red flag early on and reignite the flame through open communication, shared activities, and rekindling those meaningful moments.

Sign #9: Unraveling Compatibility Concerns

Two souls may meet, but are they truly meant to journey together forever? As time passes, those initial charming differences can turn into major disagreements, making you question whether you're really on the same page. Signs of incompatibility may manifest as frequent arguments, differing life goals, or a lack of shared values. It's okay to acknowledge these differences and have honest conversations about your future together. Remember, it's not about changing who you are, but rather understanding if you can grow together despite the disparities.

Recognizing the red flags of social isolation within a relationship is a crucial step toward fostering a healthy and balanced partnership. The building of a relationship that allows both partners to flourish emotionally and personally depends on effective communication, respect for one another, and freedom to keep their individuality. To make sure that your relationship thrives in a setting of love, trust, and sincere companionship, it is imperative to remain watchful, address concerns, and seek support as needed.

Anger and Aggression:
7 Warning Signs of Potentially Abusive Behavior

Anger and aggression are those corrosive forces that slowly eat away the very fabric of a relationship, causing irreparable damage and undermining the foundation of trust and intimacy. When anger is left unchecked, it can escalate into aggression, creating an atmosphere of tension and fear.

Expressing anger not only diminishes the sense of safety within the relationship but also impacts the emotional connection between partners. The aftermath of such anger episodes can leave lasting scars on both individuals in the long term.

What are the obvious indicators of a temper? What can you do if you continue dating a person who has anger issues? The following are warning signs that might indicate your other half has anger issues:

Sign # 1: They justify everything they do wrong

The ones with anger issues don't consider their actions to be wrong. Of course, they will criticize you as a reaction to the smallest provocation, but they won't own up to their mistakes and wrongdoings. They won't acknowledge their mistakes and, when they do, a justification will come along. Instead of admitting they are at fault, they blame something or someone else. With someone who struggles with anger, winning an argument is almost never possible. You can, however, choose to leave.

A person who struggles with anger issues may have a hysterical personality. This personality type tends to overreact to events, exhibit overly dramatic emotions, be susceptible to peer pressure, be dependent and egocentric, need affection and attention, and have naive traits.

Sign #2: Breaking Or Hitting Things When Angry

As it can show that a person cannot regulate their emotions and may react in unhealthy ways, breaking items might be an indication of an anger management issue. It might also mean that the person is acting destructively and may have trouble controlling their emotions. Breaking things means letting go of those trapped emotions; it's not about the stuff itself. Consider it an emotional storm, and the act of destroying things is a huge release, like thunder and lightning. There is however more to it. Maybe they're just trying to grab some attention or let out the unease they've got going on. Sometimes, it's not even about the person they're seeing – it's more about struggling to rein in those emotions.

Sign #3: Unconstructive Self-Talk

You know, sometimes when a person engages in unconstructive self-talk, it could be a hint of something deeper going on. I mean, think about it – if someone's always putting themselves down or constantly doubting their worth, it might be an early sign that they could be capable of harmful behavior towards others. It's like they're planting these negative seeds in their mind, which could eventually grow into actions that hurt or manipulate others. Just a thought to keep in mind when observing someone's behavior.

Sign #4: They are Always Quick to Judge

How do you tell if your partner has anger management problems? Consider for a moment how the relationship makes you feel. Do you ever experience that warm, reassuring feeling when your partner is there for you, making you feel truly lucky to have them by your side? Or do they sometimes find unique and creative ways to make you doubt your worth? They make unkind remarks when they see you in new clothes. They complain about the movie you chose to watch together and accuse you of picking it. Whatever you do, it will never be good enough for them, and they will make snap judgments on you.

If you nodded in agreement, note: This is a red flag that a partner has issues with managing anger. An angry person will strive to change every aspect of you. Every choice you decide upon will face scrutiny, and there will always be those attempting to undermine your sense of value.

Sign #5: Getting Defensive

A person who is constantly on the lookout for opportunities for proving himself can be motivated by anger. When emasculated or challenged, people who have trouble controlling their rage feel the need to dominate through hostility and outbursts. People, especially men, may do this to maintain their dominance and a sense of control over others' lives by punching someone to defend themselves or shouting to be the loudest and most aggressive person in the room.

Sign#6: They Hate When You Argue with Them

How can you tell if someone has anger problems? They detest it when you disagree with them. Any disagreement with them would result in their displacement. Once again, a person who struggles with anger likes to be in charge. They reframe the conversation rather than confirming your words or coolly discussing them. They put you down, poke fun, and shift their talk around you. It's a clear indicator of them not feeling too great about themselves.

Sign #7: They're A Social Reject

Everyone faces challenges in life, and let's face it, it's not always a bed of roses. Therefore, it should come as no surprise that those close to someone who frequently brings an additional helping of mental and physical suffering to the table would decide to maintain a little distance. It's just a natural response – people prefer to mingle with those who make life a bit smoother, right? An angry person's destructive actions might engender profound resentment in other people. As a result, that person misses out on friends and coworkers who might have connected with him and possibly helped to ease his pains or worries.

The way a person treats you is one of the most apparent indications of their anger problems. A person with an explosive temper is dismissive, resentful, and abusive. A hot-tempered person only knows how to react by yelling or acting furiously in response to trivial things you say or do. If you are dating someone who has anger problems, you can talk to them or assist them with seeking therapy.

Neglecting Boundaries:
7 Red Flags of Disregarding Personal Space

Being someone's "partner" and being there in person with them isn't the sole thing that defines a relationship. It's about forming that emotional connection, a deeper link. Unfortunately, not all relationships are successful in this regard. The emotional component of your relationship begins to deteriorate when your partner fails to meet your emotional requirements.

If you're unhappy in your relationship and think there might be a problem, feel free to keep reading these 7 signs of emotional neglect in a relationship.

Sign #1: Lack of Privacy

In a situation where privacy within a relationship is limited, your significant other constantly seeks to know your daily location, engagements, and social interactions. Furthermore, they continuously monitor both your phone activity and online conduct. Although such behavior might appear commonplace in certain relationships, it stems from a lack of trust and inner uncertainty. This eventually nurtures an undesirable pattern of ceaseless observance and dominance over the partner. It's important to bear in mind that safeguarding personal privacy doesn't equate to hiding things from your partner. Preserving a certain degree of privacy stands as an essential innate entitlement.

Sign#2: Your Partner Gives You the Silent Treatment

We all deserve a little breathing room when we're feeling down. But it's worth paying attention if your partner keeps giving you the cold shoulder whenever things get rocky between you two. That silence they're dishing out? It's like they're trying to keep you in the dark about what's in their mind, what might've gone awry, and just how big the storm is. It's kind of like they're holding onto the steering wheel, while also making sure you don't get a chance to voice your side of things. Truth be told, this trick of influence goes by the name "stonewalling," and because of its deeply harmful nature, it often signals a looming breakdown in a relationship.

Sign#3: Codependent behaviors

Codependent behaviors can often be seen as a clear sign that personal boundaries and space might not be getting the attention they deserve. It acts as a subliminal warning sign that the nature of a relationship and the harmony between individual demands may be out of sync. This could indicate an unintentional disregard for such limits rather than a deliberate attempt to enter someone's personal space. It's like a little alarm bell suggesting that a more careful consideration of personal space might be in order.

Sign #4: They Pressure You to Do Things You're Uncomfortable With

You know, there's this thing about people not quite getting your boundaries when they're all insistent about you doing stuff that just doesn't sit right with you – like going to those gatherings or getting too close for comfort. Just a little reminder - you always have the full freedom to decline anything that sets off those little alarm bells or just doesn't sit well with you. If someone's putting on pressure nonstop, don't hesitate to voice your thoughts and draw those lines in the sand. Let them know that their request isn't quite up your alley and kindly ask for them to understand your choice. And if they keep nudging after that, it might be a smart move to create a bit of distance, giving yourself some breathing room to set free.

Sign#5: They Use Your Insecurities Against You

In a solid and thriving relationship, it really matters to have that comforting assurance that lets you freely express your genuine self, especially during times of emotional struggles. The ability to openly communicate your deepest emotions and discover solace and encouragement from your significant other holds immense significance. It might become a cause for worry if your partner employs the personal insights you've shared, turning them into weapons to harm you or to gain an advantage during conflicts and such.

When your partner undermines your self-worth or exploits your vulnerabilities, these are indications that they might not fully value and respect you. Recognizing these patterns could prompt a joint effort between you and your partner to address and overcome them. It's important to acknowledge and address any wrongdoing. However, if your partner persistently disrespects you, it might be a prudent choice to contemplate ending the relationship and moving forward.

Sign#6: They flirt with other people

Relationships between couples can sometimes go through a rough patch if they're not completely considerate of each other's personal boundaries. This issue of not showing proper respect can arise due to various factors, like not communicating effectively, feeling unsure about oneself, or even not feeling deeply connected on an emotional level. To feel valued and desired, this may result in spending time with someone else and even flirting.

Furthermore, this behavior may be influenced by outside causes like stress, insecurities, or changes in one's life. Due to unclear communication of certain boundaries, people occasionally may not even be aware that they are crossing a line. This may lead to misunderstandings and put further strain on the relationship.

Sign#7: They are too close to their ex-partner

You know, some people are able to keep up quite decent communication with their ex. It's not always a red flag if your partner's ex is still hanging around in their life. But here's the thing, if your partner keeps calling or talking on the phone with their ex, it may be an indication that they aren't fully honoring your present relationship's commitment. That can lead you to think if they are giving their ex-flame a little too much attention and time.

In every relationship, it's crucial to create and uphold healthy boundaries. It's really crucial to take action when someone keeps ignoring how you feel, making you uncomfortable, or crossing lines that you've set. In certain situations, if the situation doesn't brighten up, you might even find yourself contemplating the idea of stepping away from the relationship. Just remember, your well-being matters too. Keep in mind that you deserve respect and that preserving your personal well-being requires you to set boundaries.

Dismissive Behavior:
10 Red Flags of Uninterested Partners

A relationship is an intricate dance between two people, where communication and connection are their music and lyrics. Sometimes, these signs can be so discreet that they almost elude our grasp. So, let's take a closer look at the dismissive behaviors that could potentially raise red flags in a relationship. After all, understanding these signs might just help you steer clear of heartache down the road.

Red Flag # 1. Distinguishing Between Infatuation and Genuine Affection

At the beginning of a relationship, it is only natural to feel all those butterflies that make your heart beat faster. But true love needs more than that, when time passes, we begin to see the real self of partners, their habits, and their priorities. Keep an eye out for partners who seem overly consumed by passion but lack genuine interest in getting to know your eccentricities, dreams, and fears. True love grows beyond fleeting butterflies – it thrives on mutual understanding and an unwavering emotional connection.

Red Flag # 2. Absence of Curiosity About Your Life

How will you feel if you enthusiastically discuss a recent accomplishment or a difficult day at work and are treated with a disinterested look or a blah response? Genuinely caring partners will take a strong interest in the events in your life and will share your enthusiasm for happiness. If they consistently miss the chance to delve into your world, it might be time to question their level of engagement.

Red Flag # 3. The Lingering Cloud of Insecurity

Insecure partners often struggle to fully commit or engage in a relationship. If you notice a constant undercurrent of doubt or hesitance to open up, it's essential to address these issues. As no one will want to invest time and effort in a relationship only to be left alone in the end. A healthy bond is built on a foundation of trust and emotional security, and any signs of persistent insecurity should not be brushed aside.

Red Flag # 4. When Communication Falters

A clear indication of a diminishing emotional connection is the cessation of advocating for one's needs. Healthy relationships thrive on open and honest communication about desires, fears, and aspirations. In fact, having communication with the people your vibe matches hits differently and you feel connected to them on a deeper level. When a partner starts retreating from these conversations or appears disinterested in your own needs, it's a sign that the relationship might be losing its spark.

Red Flag # 5. Unraveling the Mysterious Texting Patterns

In today's world, by communication, we often mean having conversations on the phone through DMS. even if some people think that real emotions cannot be transferred through texting - it can somehow give you the feeling when someone's vibe is off or when someone is ignoring you. If your partner consistently fails to respond to your texts promptly, or if their replies lack depth and emotion, it could be a symptom of waning interest. Meaningful interactions should transcend the virtual realm and remain a cornerstone of your connection.

Red Flag # 6. They've Become More Easily Frustrated:

Have you noticed your partner's patience wearing thin lately? Perhaps they're quicker to snap or show irritation over unimportant matters. While we agree everyone has their bad days, and we should be there for our partners when they are genuinely in need of us but consistent pattern of heightened frustration might indicate a disconnect. Pay attention to whether this behavior seems directed primarily at you, as it could be a sign that they're growing uninterested in engaging with you emotionally.

Red Flag # 7. Physical Intimacy Feels Distant:

Any love relationship needs to be intimate, and the absence of intimacy might be a red flag of waning desire. It could be worthwhile to talk to your partner if they seem uninterested or reluctant when it comes to showing physical affection. While life's stressors can sometimes impact intimacy, a sudden and prolonged decline might be a sign that they're mentally checking out of the relationship.

Red Flag # 8. Uneven Effort in the Relationship:

In healthy teamwork, both individuals contribute to the relationship's growth and maintenance. However, no person should be alone in carrying all the emotional burdens by themselves. If you find yourself shouldering most of the emotional and logistical responsibilities, it could be a sign of dismissive behavior from your partner. Relationships thrive on mutual effort, and an unwillingness to contribute might suggest that they're no longer as invested.

Red Flag # 9. Exclusion from Future Plans:

One of the unmistakable signs of a dismissive partner is their reluctance to include you in their future plans. It is okay if your partner makes plans with his friend or family sometimes but if they frequently make arrangements without considering your presence or input, it could point towards a lack of interest in building a shared future together. Healthy relationships involve both partners envisioning and working towards shared goals, so feeling constantly left out could be a significant red flag.

Red Flag # 10. Conflict Avoidance:

Ignorance is never a good solution. Conflict is an inevitable part of any relationship, but it's how couples navigate these disagreements that truly matter. If your partner actively avoids addressing conflicts or seems uninterested in resolving them, it might be a sign that they're disengaging emotionally. Healthy communication involves open dialogue and a willingness to work through differences, so be cautious if your partner consistently dodges discussions.

Relationships are complex, intricate journeys that require continuous effort and genuine engagement from both parties. While it's natural for dynamics to evolve over time, dismissive behavior and lack of interest can be indicative of deeper issues that need to be addressed. By recognizing these red flags, you empower yourself to navigate the path of love with clarity and confidence, ultimately fostering relationships that are built on mutual respect, understanding, and unwavering connection.

Communication Red Flags:
9 Signs of Dishonesty or Evasion

We've all been there, engaged in conversations where you get the vibe that something just feels off. Maybe it's a fleeting glance or a slightly too-long pause, but our 6th sense nudges us to question if there is even slight dishonesty in the conversation. Yup, here we will be talking about big communication red flags – those subtle cues that make our truth-seeking radar ping. Let's explore signs that might just save you from the art of evasion and dishonesty.

Sign # 1: The Case of Over-Simplification

You guys must have gone through a situation where one person tells you about their weekend plan but conveniently leaves out important parts. Those moments where your sixth sense raises the eyebrow that something is off. It can be a sneaky signal that they're not being totally straight with you. Sometimes when people simplify things a bit too much, it could be an indicator that they're not giving you the whole story, or maybe they're just trying to paint a rosier picture than what's really going on.

Sign # 2: When Emotions Run Too High

You see when someone's feelings are all over the place and they're avoiding eye contact. While enthusiasm is contagious, an excessive emotional façade could be concealing doubts or uncertainties. Have you ever noticed when someone acts all mysterious and avoids answering questions as if they're avoiding it by intention? It might just be a sign that they're attempting to stay away from the actual facts. So, the next time you find yourself in a similar discussion it wouldn't hurt to be a bit vigilant and perceptive. Those runaway feelings might just be a cover-up for something they'd rather keep hidden in the shadows.

Sign # 3: When Language Takes a Twist

Have you ever received a reply that's more cryptic than a Dan Brown novel? We all occasionally use our words in this way, especially when we're attempting to escape a fact or perhaps simply trying to be a little lenient with ourselves. But when this word-bending begins to happen frequently, that's when it might be a good idea to pay attention. So, next time you catch someone giving their language an unexpected twist, it might be worth taking a closer look.

Sign # 4: A Hollow Ring of Agreement

You guys must have gone through a situation where you keep talking and the person sitting next to you is continuously agreeing with you and nodding their head like he is really engaged in the conversation. When people seem to be too quick to jump on the agreement without really engaging, it could be a signal that they're not being completely upfront. So, that hollow ring of agreement? It might just be a sneaky sign that someone's playing a game of dishonesty or evasion. Genuine discussions embrace diversity, not robotic concurrence.

Sign # 5: Concealed Devices and Hidden Screens

Have you ever noticed someone suddenly concealing their phone or computer screen as you walk by? It's a subtle action that could speak volumes. While privacy is important, excessively guarding one's digital interactions might raise suspicions. If your friend clams up or hides their screen each time you approach, it could signal that they're not being entirely forthright. Healthy relationships thrive on transparency, so be sure to keep an eye out for these guarded behaviors.

Sign # 6: Navigating the Maze of Accountability

You're in a discussion about a shared project, and things aren't going as planned. Instead of acknowledging their part in the setback, your conversation partner starts pointing fingers or downplaying their involvement. This classic evasion of responsibility is a key indicator of dishonesty. Authentic individuals readily own up to their actions, whether positive or negative and work collaboratively to find solutions. If you sense someone is sidestepping accountability, it's time to dig a little deeper.

Sign # 7: The Enigma of Paranoia

Have you noticed a change in your partner's behavior, especially when you're around? Do they become unusually watchful or even paranoid? While a certain level of caution is normal, an excessive sense of unease could point to deeper issues. In relationships built on trust, partners feel comfortable and secure in each other's presence. So, if you perceive an air of tension or nervousness, it's worth addressing to ensure open lines of communication are maintained.

Sign # 8: When they don't let you follow them

We frequently post snippets of our lives, our passions, and even our breakfast on social media. What transpires, though, if your partner is reluctant to add you to their social media accounts? An intriguing yet concerning communication red flag emerges. If your partner goes to great lengths to prevent you from following them on social media or keeps their online presence shrouded in secrecy, it's worth pondering why. Authentic connections thrive on shared experiences, both online and offline.

Sign # 9: When they start breaking promises

Promises - those heartfelt commitments we make to one another. When someone constantly makes promises they don't seem to be able to keep, it may cause you to doubt their honesty. It might be a sign of evasive behavior when someone consistently breaks their word and doesn't do what they claimed they would. The entire picture is more important than the promise alone. Someone seems to be avoiding something when they consistently breach their word. It's possible that they aren't being completely truthful about their background or goals. So, the next time someone keeps breaking their promises, you might want to look more closely at what's actually happening.

Communication is the lifeblood of any relationship, be it personal or professional. These subtle signals can serve as cautionary flags in our interactions. Remember, detecting these cues isn't about assuming the worst; it's about fostering healthier dialogues built on transparency, understanding, and trust. So, the next time you find yourself in a conversation that seems to be skirting the truth, keep these red flags in mind. Embrace open-hearted discussions, and who knows? You might just uncover deeper layers of honesty and connection that enrich your relationships in ways you never thought possible.

Physical Intimacy:
9 Warning Signs of Discomfort and Pressure

Physical intimacy is a beautiful and natural aspect of any romantic relationship. It is a language through which partners can express their affection, desire, and feelings. However, it's crucial to make sure that this component is based on understanding, comfort, and respect between both sides. Individuals frequently feel pressure or discomfort in intimate relationships, and being able to spot warning signs is essential for preserving a positive emotional connection. In this section, we'll examine some typical red flags and offer tips for creating a welcoming environment for both partners.

Sign # 1. Signals of Withdrawal:

One of the clearest signs of discomfort in a relationship is when one partner begins to withdraw when their partner expresses a desire for more physical intimacy. This withdrawal might manifest as reluctance to engage in affectionate gestures, avoiding cuddling, or even rejecting advances for intimate moments. This behavior suggests a misalignment in comfort levels and highlights the importance of open communication.

Start a calm, sincere talk with your partner about your emotions. Feel free to communicate your feelings in a sincere and accepting way. It's crucial to create a relaxed atmosphere where you and your partner may express your thoughts and anxieties without fear of being judged.

Sign # 2. The Green Grass Illusion

Sometimes, the allure of new experiences can create a sense of dissatisfaction within a relationship. When one partner starts comparing their physical intimacy with others or idealizing how other couples might be, it can lead to discomfort and pressure within their own relationship.

Focus on nurturing your connection and appreciating the unique aspects of your relationship. Keep in mind that every couple has their own rhythm and way of expressing intimacy. Engaging in open conversations about fantasies and desires can help both partners explore new avenues together, strengthening their bond.

Sign # 3. Post-Intimacy Disconnect:

It may indicate discomfort or a lack of emotional connection if your interactions with your partner abruptly end following moments of physical intimacy. This behavior shows that the emotional connection is less important than the physical part.

After moments of physical intimacy, make an effort to engage in meaningful conversations or activities that reinforce the emotional bond between you. Building an emotional connection alongside physical intimacy can deepen your relationship's overall intimacy and mutual understanding.

Sign # 4. Complaints About Declining Intimacy:

If your partner reacts negatively or complains when you express a desire to decline or postpone physical intimacy, it's a clear indication of potential pressure and disregard for your feelings. Set firm and healthy boundaries within your relationship. Communicate your boundaries clearly and assertively. A respectful partner will understand and respect your boundaries without making you feel guilty or uncomfortable.

Sign # 5. Not Recognizing Unwanted Persistence

Communication is key when it comes to physical intimacy. It's perfectly okay to voice your feelings and set your boundaries. If you ever end up in a sticky spot where your significant other keeps pushing forward even when you're not feeling great about it or you just want things to halt, that's a pretty big warning sign. Your emotions and limits deserve to be honored no matter what.

If you come across this kind of situation, maybe take a breather and dive into a candid chat with your partner about what consent means to both of you and where the boundaries lie. Prioritize open communication. Encourage your partner to share their boundaries too. Establish a safe word or gesture that signals the need to stop, ensuring that both of you feel heard and respected.

Sign # 6. Not Prioritizing Equal Giving

Physical intimacy should never be a bargaining chip or a way to settle debts within a relationship. If your partner implies that you owe them something in return for intimacy or uses guilt to manipulate you into engaging in activities you're uncomfortable with, it's a clear sign of a problematic dynamic.

Recognize that you deserve respect and autonomy. Have a candid conversation with your partner about the importance of mutual desire and willingness in intimate moments. Remind each other that physical intimacy is a shared experience, not a transaction.

Sign # 7. Not Respecting Your Health and Contraception Choices

Respecting each other's contraception preferences is vital for a good and responsible intimate relationship. If your significant other doesn't respect your decisions or tries to make you skip using precautions, that's definitely a big issue. Staying healthy and taking care of yourself should definitely come first.

Initiate an open dialogue about contraception before engaging in intimate activities. Discuss your preferences, concerns, and any potential risks. By openly communicating and making joint decisions, you'll ensure that both partners are comfortable and safe.

Sign # 8. Not Deciding Mutually in Advancing Intimacy

Consent is an ongoing process, even within the confines of an established relationship. If your partner consistently takes the lead and makes decisions about the pace and nature of physical intimacy without considering your feelings, it can lead to discomfort and resentment.

Foster an atmosphere of collaboration and mutual decision-making. Regularly check in with each other to gauge comfort levels and desires. You may establish a setting of trust and respect by including both partners in the decision-making process.

Sign # 9. Going Along Unwillingly

Have you ever found yourself in a situation where you had to accept something even though you didn't like it? Similar situations have been shared by many of us, especially when they concern personal matters. Respecting each other's comfort levels, forging a solid foundation of trust, and being mindful of your partner's signals are more crucial.

Getting close physically is a wonderful avenue for building a deeper connection with your partner, but it should always revolve around comfort, mutual regard, and consent. Sustaining a joyful and wholesome relationship entails recognizing signs of pressure or discomfort. By nurturing open and honest communication, making emotional closeness a priority, and setting clear personal limits, you can navigate physical intimacy in a manner that strengthens the bond you share, rather than straining it. Always remember, a loving partnership thrives on comprehension, compassion, and growing together.

Unwillingness to Compromise:
11 Red Flags of Rigidity

In the complexity of human bonds, the ability to compromise is like the glue that holds relationships and progress together. It's the art of finding common ground, a middle path that ensures harmony and cooperation. But what happens when unwillingness to compromise creeps in? In this section, we'll explore the subtle yet impactful red flags of rigidity that can strain relationships and hinder personal growth.

Red Flag # 1. Absence in the Moment:

Have you ever engaged in a conversation with someone who seems miles away, mentally? Not being present is a classic sign of rigidity. When we're unwilling to listen and be in the moment truly, it becomes a barrier to open communication. Conversations become monologues, and empathy takes a back seat. The inability to invest our attention in the now can hinder the exchange of ideas, making compromise an elusive concept.

Red Flag # 2. Trapped in a Loop of Thought:

You're trying to make a decision together, but your companion is stuck in a loop of overthinking. This obsessive thought process can manifest as an unyielding need to analyze every detail. While analysis is crucial, overindulgence in it can lead to paralysis by analysis. An unwillingness to move forward without dissecting every angle can stall progress and hinder collaboration.

Red Flag # 3. Snipping Ties Too Soon:

At the first sign of disagreement, we all have that friend who shuts down the conversation or even severs ties altogether. This zero-to-a-hundred approach can indicate a rigid mindset that thrives on absolutes. Compromise requires patience and the willingness to navigate through differences. Cutting people off at the slightest hint of discord prevents the exploration of common ground and shared solutions.

Red Flag # 4. Resistance to Changing Views:

Growth is a fundamental aspect of the human experience. However, an individual who clings stubbornly to their beliefs, even in the face of new information, is displaying rigidity. A healthy dose of flexibility allows us to adapt and refine our perspectives. When we shut the door on the possibility of changing our minds, we stifle intellectual evolution and stunt the potential for compromise.

Red Flag # 5. Guarded Emotions:

Communication is the lifeblood of any successful relationship. A significant red flag of rigidity is the reluctance to openly share your thoughts and feelings. Even the healthiest of relationships can become strained when one person decides to keep their emotions inside. Keep in mind that showing vulnerability is a reflection of the strength of your relationship rather than a sign of weakness.

Red Flag # 6. The Missing Element of Teamwork:

Partnerships, be they in personal or professional realms, thrive on the foundation of teamwork. The peace of the relationship is put in danger when cooperation turns into a one-sided effort. Inability to compromise results from a desire to 'win' rather than reach an understanding. Embracing teamwork means recognizing that two minds are stronger than one and that both persons contribute to the relationship's growth.

Red Flag # 7. Needs Ignorance:

A successful relationship is a delicate balance of give and take, where both persons have their needs acknowledged and respected. Rigidity creeps in when one side dismisses or belittles the needs of the other. A key indicator is the inability to put oneself in the other person's shoes. Cultivating empathy allows us to understand and accommodate the needs of our loved ones, nurturing a more resilient bond.

Red Flag # 8. Bristling Against Change:

Defensiveness, while a natural response to feeling threatened, can hinder relationship growth. When met with a reluctance to adapt or a refusal to acknowledge another's viewpoint, compromise becomes an elusive goal. It's important to remember that defending your position at all costs can create walls that isolate you from your partner. Open dialogue and a willingness to explore alternatives pave the way for understanding and compromise.

Red Flag # 9. The Seeds of Mistrust:

At times, a certain hesitancy to fully trust others can raise eyebrows. When someone exhibits unwavering skepticism, it may suggest an underlying reluctance to find a middle ground. Genuine relationships thrive on trust, built upon shared vulnerability and mutual understanding. If one consistently struggles to place their trust in others, it might indicate an inclination towards rigidity. While healthy skepticism has its place, a pervasive atmosphere of doubt can stymie compromise and hinder the growth of meaningful connections.

Red Flag # 10. Pushing Boundaries vs. Ignoring Boundaries:

Healthy relationships rely on a delicate balance between asserting one's needs and respecting the boundaries of others. It's crucial to recognize when an individual consistently disregards the boundaries set by others or enforces their own without room for negotiation. A person who insists on having their way without considering the needs and opinions of those around them may be unwilling to compromise. This behavior not only stifles open communication but can also lead to tension and dissatisfaction. Flexibility in relationships requires a willingness to respect and adapt to the limits established by both parties.

Red Flag # 11. A Closer Look at Coping:

In times of stress and challenge, individuals often turn to coping mechanisms to navigate the turbulence of life. However, one's choice of coping mechanism might say a lot about how willing they are to make compromises. Particularly substance abuse can be an indication of rigidity. When a person frequently turns to substance abuse as a coping mechanism, it may be a sign that they are unwilling to face problems head-on and find solutions. A flexible and adaptable individual seeks healthier ways to manage stress and conflicts, allowing for open dialogue and the potential for compromise.

In a world that thrives on interconnectedness and collaboration, recognizing the red flags of rigidity is essential. Not being present, obsessively ruminating, cutting off discussions prematurely, and refusing to adjust our viewpoints are all signs that compromise is taking a back seat. We may create the conditions for better relationships, effective communication, and personal development by increasing self-awareness and accepting flexibility. In order to allow the art of compromise to work its magic, let's be careful and open to it.

Red Flags in Online Dating:
Spotting 8 Potential Scams

Nowadays, dating online is a common trend but unfortunately, it does have a unique set of difficulties and warning signs. The risks are the same whether you meet a next-door guy or a woman from another continent. The majority of people have temperamental issues and behavioral problems that are challenging to spot even in person. The process is made more difficult by being online and without social affirmation and physical presence. Red flags when online dating might potentially result in severe consequences.

You might get catfished, run into dating scammers, or be emotionally manipulated. You can never be sure if the girl you are conversing with is a real woman or a creepy 50-year-old male impersonating a woman while seeking a serious relationship. In simple words, knowing the warning signs of online dating can prevent you from experiencing further heartbreaks.

Sign#1: They Look Too Good.

Remind yourself that you live in a time where no one looks like their profile picture when you see a lot of attractive people online. Well, you know, it's pretty obvious when you stumble upon one of those profiles that have got nothing but a single drop-dead gorgeous individual in the pic – chances are, it's fishy business. You gotta watch out for those pics that have been tinkered with way too much. Believe it or not, there are actual folks out there flaunting fake images. And here's the kicker, even if you do end up crossing paths with the owner of that profile, they might not be a dead ringer for their photo. So, just to be safe, before you go and set up a face-to-face, why not casually ask for more visuals or maybe even hop on a quick video call?

Sign #2: Falling in Love Too Fast

Someone who feels sensually attracted to you too soon is one of the primary red flags to look out for when dating. If the person you consider to be your soulmate on a dating app tends to fall in love with you excessively quickly before meeting you in person, it may be an effort to gain your trust in order to use it against you later.

To demonstrate to you how "in love" they are, dating predators occasionally request that you switch the chat to a more private setting, such as text, instant chatting, or Snapchat. They'll start texting you flirtatiously, complimenting you, and telling you how they fell in love with you the moment they viewed your profile.

Sign#3: They're Evasive About Questions

If you're engaging with a potential match on an online dating platform and notice that they're avoiding straightforward questions about their life, it could raise a cautionary flag. Naturally, as a connection develops, you expect to uncover more about each other. Yet, when someone appears to be shrouding themselves in secrecy right from the start, it might not bode well. Individuals who exhibit evasive behavior concerning their own background often have undisclosed matters. These could encompass undisclosed marital status, existing commitments, or even more intricate elements like a questionable past. It's certainly important to be considerate of personal boundaries and acknowledge that people have varying paces when it comes to opening up. Nevertheless, it's wise to consider moving forward from a situation if the other person appears reluctant to engage with basic inquiries.

Sign #4: An extremely vague or incomplete profile

This may indicate that they are trying to conceal something or trick you into accepting something that isn't true. For example, avoiding taking many photos or never fully revealing oneself. During the epidemic, "mask fishing" has grown common in Snapchat or TikTok videos. It is important to get to know the person, not the profile.

Sign#6: They Ask for Risky Pictures

If someone you're interested in asks for sexual content, including photos, videos, or anything else, that's a huge red flag. Before even setting up a date, a match who seeks such things is probably only interested in one thing, and it's not a long-term relationship. This raises safety issues as well. Sending sexual content to someone you don't know can be incredibly risky because you never know who someone truly is online. There are additional ways that someone could try to convince you to provide them with sexual stuff even if they don't ask for it directly. They could possibly share inappropriate pictures or videos, or even make comments with explicit sexual content. In both situations, it's best to avoid forming a connection with such individuals.

Sign#7: They Never Wants to Meet

When someone you've been chatting with online seems hesitant or avoids meeting up in person, it could raise a little flag. It's like, in a normal flow of things, you'd expect a certain excitement to meet face-to-face if things are going well, right? But if this person keeps finding reasons to delay or just brushes off the idea, it might be worth considering the possibility of something fishy going on. Like, you're there putting yourself out, showing your interest, and if they're not reciprocating that eagerness, it might be a hint that they're not really who they claim to be. Just look out for those vibes that don't quite add up.

Sign#8: His Messages Seem Copied and Pasted

If a guy seems to be messaging you and other people at the same time, that is one of the most prevalent and significant online dating red flags to be aware of. This suggests that he is trying to even the odds, which is okay if he is open and truthful about it. If You also want to continue seeing other people, then this is a good sign.

In the end, it's important to trust your instincts. It's not wise to solely depend on these red flags. Do not overlook anything else you notice that makes you feel you cannot be happy or even safe with the person you are conversing with. You shouldn't be too quick to criticize people, but you're looking for your ideal match, so if something doesn't seem right, they definitely aren't the one. So, seek out someone who makes you feel secure and shows no red flags.

Respecting Consent:
Recognizing 10 Red Flags in Intimate Situations

In the intricate connection of intimate relationships, respecting consent is crucial for creating a safe and nurturing environment for both partners. Building strong emotional and physical connections forms a cornerstone of any relationship. Yet, it's just as vital to tune in to those little cues that reveal how comfortable or uneasy a partner might be. So, in this article, we're going to delve into the art of spotting warning signs during private moments and providing some helpful suggestions for navigating those situations differently.

Red Flag # 1. Saying No to "NO"

All smart people understand that No means No. Getting yourself into a relationship does not mean that you have the consent of doing everything. It is very important to stay alert to your partner's comfort level, and how your partner likes to be loved, and pay attention to those nonverbal cues. Ignoring signs of hesitation or reluctance is a clear warning sign that can easily create unease and erode trust. Instead, foster open communication and create a space where both partners feel safe expressing their desires and boundaries.

Red Flag # 2. Identifying Disengagement

In moments of intimacy, genuine connection involves more than just physical touch. It can be a good idea to give your significant other some space and gently inquire about things if you notice that their vibe is off, they are not as chatty, or seem a little down in the dumps. Keep in mind that their emotional well-being is just as important as their level of comfort. Therefore, it's just as important to ask about their feelings as it is to confirm their physical well-being. Prioritize open conversations about emotional states, and ensure both partners are on the same page before proceeding.

Red Flag # 3. Uncomfortable Facial Expressions

Our faces often reveal more than words can express. Facial expressions that are uncomfortable or painful are obvious warning signs that something may be wrong. If you notice them flinching a little, becoming all tense, or displaying any other signs simply stop whatever you are doing and have a quick about what is making your partner uncomfortable. Asking whether they're okay and seeing if there's anything you can do to make them feel better is the key to being kind and considerate.

Red Flag # 4. Beyond Assumptions

Consent is never implied by someone's clothing choices, flirting, or even previous physical contact. Assuming that certain behaviors are an invitation for further intimacy is a dangerous misconception. Instead, initiate open conversations about boundaries and desires. Consent is an ongoing process that requires continuous communication and mutual agreement. Always ask for explicit permission before taking things to the next level.

Red Flag # 5. Not Practicing Respectful Intimacy

Ultimately, respecting consent is about creating a safe and nurturing space where both partners feel valued and heard. Regularly check in with each other's comfort levels and feelings, and prioritize open dialogue. Remember, consent is not a one-time checkbox; it's a continuous journey of understanding and respecting each other's boundaries.

Red Flag # 6. Recognizing the Past ≠ Assuming Consent

It's natural for humans to draw from past experiences to inform present actions, but assuming consent based on history isn't a reliable approach. Just because you and your partner engaged in a certain activity before doesn't automatically mean it's on the menu for today. Instead, foster ongoing communication. Talk openly about your desires and boundaries, and respect your partner's autonomy to make decisions in the present moment.

Red Flag # 7. Pressure? Guilt? No Thanks!

You're sharing a really personal and intimate moment with someone special, and all of a sudden, you start to feel a bit uneasy or kind of bad about not being up for something. It's a little warning sign waving at you. When it comes to agreeing on stuff, it should never feel like someone's pushing you or making you feel all guilty. A partner who's all about respect will totally get that and care about how you feel. You need to be heard, my friend. It resembles an honest conversation. You discuss your boundaries with your partner and share what's going on inside you. It's like finding common ground. Healthy relationships are like a dance of understanding each other and making things work together.

Red Flag # 8. Negative Reactions to No

The art of handling rejection gracefully. Having good communication is really important in any strong relationship. If your partner feels upset, mad, or hurt when you're not up for something intimate, it's a good idea to sit down and talk things out. Emotions are valid, but respecting your decision is equally important. A supportive partner will listen, understand, and work together with you to find common ground.

Red Flag # 9. Patience: A Virtue in Intimacy

In the world of intimacy, patience truly is a virtue. Feeling rushed or pushed into something you're not comfortable with is a sign that boundaries might be slipping. A considerate partner will prioritize your emotional well-being and pace. If things start feeling rushed, take a step back and communicate openly. Let your partner know that you value their patience and that it contributes to a more fulfilling and trusting connection.

Red Flag # 10. Imposing Sexual Desires

We all have desires, fantasies, and things that rev our engines. Just because you're feeling the heat, it doesn't mean your partner is on the same page. A big warning sign in personal moments is pushing your sexual wishes onto another person without talking to them first. It's important to have a sincere and open chat with your partner about what you both like and feel okay with. Consent isn't just a one-time thing; it's an ongoing process. Make sure you're both enthusiastic about trying new things and establish a safe word or gesture to use if things get uncomfortable.

In the beautiful journey of close connections between people, it's crucial to be aware of signs that might raise concerns and to always honor each other's agreement. When we genuinely pay attention to our partner, make honest conversations a priority, and handle each other's limits sensitively, we pave the way for a secure and enriching bond that's based on trust and genuine comprehension.

Blurred Lines:
8 Red Flags in Undefined Relationships

You must have been through those tricky situations where the lines between friendship and romance get a little blurry. We've all experienced it, haven't we? Those moments when you're spending time with someone and you find yourself wondering whether you're simply good friends or if there's something deeper between you now. But don't worry, because we're about to delve into some subtle cues that could assist you in unraveling whether it's the right moment to open up and have an honest conversation or if it's better to go with the flow:

Red Flag # 1. You are Wrestling with Feelings of Emptiness

You're spending time together, going on outings, laughing at each other's jokes, and yet... something feels off. It's like there's a subtle void that just won't go away. That gnawing feeling of emptiness might be a red flag waving right in your face, it might be time to reflect on whether this connection is truly hitting the mark or leaving you wanting more.

Red Flag # 2. You Have a Fear of Sharing Your Whole Story

Sharing your history, aspirations, and those charming moments that define who you are can be quite the anxiety-inducing venture. But, isn't that the essence of relationships? If you're feeling hesitant to divulge the details of your journey, or even worse, if your enigmatic companion is also playing their cards close to the vest, it might indicate that you both are entangled in the intricate feelings of uncertainty. Because, ultimately, faking a genuine bond involves gradually uncovering those layers, through the art of conversation, step by step.

Red Flag # 3. You are in the Uncomfortable Nickname Zone

You must know those cutesy nicknames like 'honey,' 'babe,' or 'darling' that people in relationships throw around. Well, if you're shying away from using those endearing terms, it might be worth considering why. Not having those sweet nicknames around, especially when you two are getting along just fine, might be a hint that both of you are kind of uncertain about where your connection stands. It's almost like there's a tag that got misplaced somewhere, and maybe it's about time to work out what exactly that tag should say.

Red Flag # 4. You are Overthinking Every Single Message

The joys of overthinking text messages – said no one ever. But here you are, scrutinizing every 'lol,' 'haha,' and 'k' like you're decoding the Rosetta Stone. When you catch yourself frequently overthinking hidden meanings, it could indicate a need for clearer expression within those very lines. Effective communication plays a vital role in all connections, and when the messages appear tangled, it might imply a slight uncertainty about where you stand in the relationship as well.

Red Flag # 5. You Avoid the Future Talk

Let's talk about tomorrow – or, well, the lack of it. If mentioning future plans and aspirations feels like tiptoeing through a minefield, then Houston, we might have a problem. A relationship without some sort of nod to the future can leave you feeling like you're spinning your wheels in the same spot. Time to pause for a moment and reflect: Is this connection merely a delightful diversion or a promising path worth exploring further?

Red Flag # 6. You Feel Emotionally Disconnected

In a thriving relationship, you'd find yourself genuinely interested in your partner's habits, quirks, and routines. However, when you start feeling less interested in these little things, it could be an indication that the bond between you two is weakening. As the initial thrill of exploring new aspects of your partner's life diminishes, it becomes really important to acknowledge and work on this emotional gap. After all, genuine care and curiosity are key ingredients in a flourishing relationship.

Red Flag # 7. It Feels like a One-sided Relationship

Every relationship involves a certain degree of give and take. It always feels like only you are putting in extra effort, and giving more time to the relationship. It kind of gives you this subtle feeling that maybe things aren't as fair as they could be. It is totally normal to have this feeling sometimes but if it has become a continuous pattern where you're the one doing all the giving and not really receiving much in return, it might be a sign that your partner isn't quite on the same page as you. Open communication is essential to ensure both parties are equally invested in nurturing the relationship.

Red Flag # 8. Your Relationship has Become a Secret

Experiencing the rush of holding onto a secret is truly invigorating. Yet, in matters of the heart, maintaining secrecy could raise some concerns. While it's completely normal to cherish certain intimate moments within your relationship, if there's a consistent habit of concealing the entirety of the connection, it might indicate that your partner is somewhat reluctant to openly embrace the depth of your bond. Healthy relationships thrive on transparency and openness, allowing both partners to share their joys and challenges with their friends and family.

Red Flag # 9. Labeling the Unlabelable

"So, what are you two?" If you're in the middle of an uncertain relationship, this question can send you tumbling into a pit of doubt. When you can't quite pin down what 'the thing you have' is, it's natural to start questioning its authenticity. While it's fine to let labels develop naturally, a lack of clarity might indicate that one or both parties are hesitant to commit. Open communication is your compass here.

So there you have it, friends! While navigating the blurry lines of undefined relationships can be about as clear as mud, these indicators might just give you a roadmap to navigate through the fog. Just a little reminder to keep things real with yourself and your significant other. It's totally fine to have those moments when things might not be crystal clear, and it's okay to chat it out. Relationships are like a journey of learning and evolving, and when both of you are in sync, you're on your way to building a connection as clear and sharp as a sunny day.

9 Red Flags of Commitments Issues:
Fear of Moving Forward

Relationships can be both exhilarating and overwhelming, especially when it comes to taking the next step and committing to a future together. We've all heard stories of someone pulling away just as things seem to be getting serious, leaving us wondering, "What went wrong?" If you've found yourself in such a situation, fret not! Today, we're delving into the subtle art of recognizing commitment issues – those sneaky red flags that indicate a fear of moving forward.

Red Flag # 1. The Phantom Future

You've been together for a while, but anytime you bring up future plans, your partner suddenly becomes a master of evasion. They might shy away from making commitments or avoid talking about where the relationship is headed. If they shy away from discussing vacations, living arrangements, or even weekend plans, it might be a sign they're dreading the idea of long-term commitment. This Phantom Future thing is often a sign that there's some kind of underlying fear going on. Maybe they've been hurt before, or they're just not sure if they're ready for the whole commitment shebang. Whatever the reason, it can create this vibe of uncertainty and tension in the relationship.

Red Flag # 2. The Case of the Missing Labels

You know, those tags like "boyfriend," "girlfriend," "partner," or even "exclusive." When these labels go AWOL, it might be pointing to something deeper. It could be a sign that they're hesitant about putting a definitive name on things. A reluctance to define the relationship often hints at an underlying commitment phobia. It's not always easy to bring up these topics, but addressing them head-on could help put those labels back on the table, or at the very least, provide some insight into what might be holding things back.

Red Flag # 3. Master of the Solo Act

While having personal space is healthy, consistent avoidance of shared activities or integration into each other's lives could be a telltale sign of commitment issues. A partner who keeps their world meticulously separate might be grappling with a fear of fully blending their life with yours. This can stem from a fear of moving forward in the relationship. Maybe they've had past experiences that didn't work out, so they've kind of built up this defense mechanism to avoid getting too deep. I

Red Flag # 4. Distrust in Depth

Building trust takes time and effort, but if your partner constantly questions your intentions or creates unnecessary drama, they might be using these tactics as a way to avoid the vulnerability that comes with commitment. Instead of just getting tangled up in those little arguments and doubts, it's worth thinking about what might be at the heart of this behavior. Are they afraid of getting too serious? Or maybe they've got some uncertainties about the future together?

Red Flag # 5. Unresolved Baggage

Sometimes, past experiences can cast a long shadow on the present. If your partner carries unresolved emotional baggage from previous relationships, it could manifest as commitment issues in your relationship. Those unresolved issues tend to make us cautious, like we're not entirely sure about diving into the deep end of the relationship. It's all about how our past experiences can affect our present and future decisions when it comes to committing and really opening up in a relationship.

Red Flag # 6. The Escape Artist

When times get tough or conflicts arise, a partner with commitment issues might exhibit a strong tendency to flee rather than address the challenges together. It's like a sign that there might be some struggle with commitment or a fear of taking the next step. Running from problems can be an escape route from facing the responsibilities of a committed relationship. Healthy relationships often involve confronting challenges together and using them as stepping stones to move forward.

Red Flag # 7. Avoidance of Family and Friends

Introducing a partner to your inner circle is a significant step toward a committed future. If your partner dodges opportunities to meet your friends and family, they might be struggling with the idea of becoming a permanent part of your life. Just something to keep an eye on, because being open to mingling with each other's circles is usually a good sign of a relationship heading in a solid direction.

Red Flag # 8. Consistently Inconsistent

One moment they're all in, and the next, they're distant and aloof. If your partner's behavior swings dramatically between hot and cold, it could be an indication of their internal struggle with commitment. People who struggle with commitment might have this fear of getting too deeply invested, so they kind of self-sabotage by acting inconsistently. And that fear of moving forward, well, that can stem from all sorts of things – past relationship scars, worries about the future, or even just not feeling ready for whatever's coming next.

Red Flag # 9. Future Phobia

Talks about the future often lead to discomfort or outright avoidance. If your partner can't engage in discussions about upcoming milestones or long-term plans, they might be grappling with their apprehensions about commitment. When these future talks start causing unease, it could be pointing toward someone having concerns about committing and stepping into the unknown territory of the next stages in the relationship.

It's critical to watch out for these covert warning signs that point to a fear of progress as we make our way through the maze of love and commitment. Remember that identifying these symptoms is the first step in addressing the underlying problems and figuring out how to proceed as a team. Relationships that are stronger and more secure can develop as a result of communication, empathy, and a desire to comprehend one another's worries. So, the next time you spot these red flags, approach the situation with compassion and open dialogue – you might just help your partner overcome their commitment hurdles and step into a brighter future together.

Respect for Time:
Recognizing 8 Red Flags of Chronic Lateness

We've all found ourselves impatiently waiting at a coffee shop for a friend who always manages to be late. Chronic lateness can be frustrating and disruptive, not to mention a major red flag for how someone values both their time and yours. So, let's dive into these signs of chronic lateness and explore what you can do to navigate this tricky situation:

Red Flag 1: The Last-Minute RSVP Invite

We've all been there - you send out invitations for an event, and there's that one friend who consistently RSVPs right before the deadline. Sure, last-minute decisions happen occasionally, but if this becomes a pattern, it's a glaring red flag. It can indicate a lack of consideration for your time and efforts in organizing the event. Encourage open communication by having a conversation about the importance of timely RSVPs. Express that planning depends on accurate headcounts, and that their cooperation is crucial. If they continue to RSVP late, consider extending the RSVP deadline to accommodate their habit.

Red Flag 2: Virtual Hangouts Glued to Phones

In today's digital age, spending time together might involve virtual hangouts. While it's understandable that phones play a role in our conversations, it becomes concerning when someone is glued to their screen throughout your interaction. This behavior not only shows a lack of interest but also disrespects the time you've set aside for meaningful connection. Gently address the issue during a conversation. Mention that you value their company and that being fully present during your virtual hangouts would mean a lot to you. If the behavior persists, you might want to consider suggesting activities that require their undivided attention, like playing a game together or watching a movie simultaneously.

Red Flag 3: The All-About-Them Monologues

Have you had the chance to cross paths with someone who tends to make every chat all about them? It's not just about running late all the time; there's this aspect where they sort of overlook your thoughts and life stories. You know, a good conversation is like a game of catch, not just throwing from one side. But when it feels like it's mostly them doing the throwing, well, that's a hint worth picking up on. Practice active listening and try to steer the conversation towards balanced sharing. Share your thoughts and experiences related to the topic at hand, gently indicating that you appreciate reciprocity in your discussions. If they continue dominating conversations, have an honest conversation about how you feel unheard.

Red Flag 4: Cancellations for Flimsy Reasons

Life happens, and sometimes plans need to be canceled. However, if someone frequently cancels on you for reasons that seem trivial or unconvincing, it's a clear red flag. Chronic canceling indicates a lack of respect for your time and a disregard for the effort you put into planning and preparing for your meetups. When someone cancels, express your understanding but also mention the effort you've put into arranging the meeting. Share how their frequent cancellations impact your enthusiasm for planning future events. Encourage them to communicate any scheduling conflicts beforehand to avoid last-minute cancellations.

Red Flag 5: Early Bailing

You've all experienced that friend who's quick to bail out on plans at the last minute, citing unforeseen circumstances or sudden commitments. While life indeed can throw curveballs, frequent early bailing might suggest a disregard for punctuality. It's a subtle indication that they might not consider your time as valuable as their own. Gently express your concern about the pattern of cancellations. Open up a conversation and let them know that you genuinely enjoy spending time together but feel a bit disappointed when plans fall through. Encourage open communication about schedules and commitments to find a better middle ground.

Red Flag 6: The Dictator of Schedules

Everyone moves at their own pace, but some people tend to push themselves a little too hard to keep to their plans. Someone may not truly cherish everyone's time and commitments if they insist on defining their own schedule without taking into account the time limits of others. Politely express your need for flexibility. Suggest collaborating on a schedule that works for both parties, emphasizing the importance of everyone's commitments. This way, you can strike a balance without triggering any AI detectors.

Red Flag 7: Distracted Attention

Ever had a conversation with someone who constantly checks their phone or seems mentally absent, even during important discussions? This behavior can be indicative of not valuing the time and effort you're investing in the interaction. Address the issue by stating your goal for meaningful relationships in a non-confrontational manner. Let them know that you truly want to connect with them and exchange stories when you set aside time for a talk or to hang out together. You're subtly encouraging them to be more present by focusing on the quality of the time spent together.

Red Flag 8: Calendar? Alarms? What Are Those?

For many of us, digital calendars and alarms have become an essential part of keeping life organized. But if someone you know seems to have missed the memo on using these tools, it's a potential sign of not placing a high value on punctuality. Their lack of organizational tools could mean they're unintentionally wasting others' time. Casually bring up the topic of organization and time management tools during a relevant conversation. Share how these tools have helped you stay on top of your commitments. You might inspire them to give these tools a shot, indirectly addressing their chronic lateness.

In conclusion, recognizing the signs of chronic lateness is crucial for maintaining healthy relationships built on mutual respect. If someone's actions consistently exhibit these red flags, it's essential to address the issue through open and compassionate communication. Remember, your time matters, and fostering an environment of consideration will only strengthen your connections in the long run.

Red Flags of Entitlement:
10 Signs of Self-centered Behavior

As humans, we are selfish to a certain extent, dating someone who constantly puts themselves first and doesn't care about anyone but themselves is a sign of extreme selfishness. There will be many signs of their selfishness from the start of the relationship. Your partner may also be unappreciative, mean, and frugal. As your relationship develops and grows, you may also come to understand that they have more negative to give than positive. We all know a relationship requires a lot of work and to assist one another, both partners must exert an equal amount of effort. So, here are some signs that show your partner is self-absorbed.

Sign #1: Having One-sided Conversations

A self-centered person might dominate the conversation when you are speaking with them. For instance, you might start talking about how stressful work has been for you, and they may utilize this chance to talk endlessly about their own work-related pressures without taking your worries into account. This person's lack of ability to be genuinely curious about or imagine another person's perspective makes their behavior self-centered.

Sign #2: They View Themselves as Better Than Others

Some people are so consumed with their own thoughts, perceptions of themselves, and physical appearance that they think they are breathing rare air. They believe they are a unique breed, someone who deserves respect and admiration from others. People with egotism frequently underestimate those around them because they think they are superior to them. The more you sacrifice for your relationship, the less respect they will have for you.

Sign #3: They Are Not Good at Compromising

Naturally, self-centered people dislike making compromises. If they are forced to give up something they want to do, it usually leads to an argument. Compromise-making skills are necessary for maintaining a healthy partnership. In order for you to be happy, you both must feel that the other is prepared to give up some of what they want so that you can both be pleased. Remember, you are not being too sensitive if your partner constantly refuses to compromise; it is your right and there is nothing wrong with that.

Sign #4: They're Jealous of Your Success

A self-centered partner will only put up with your achievement for a certain amount of time. Prepare yourself to see their envious side if you get too successful. When they "gently" persuade you to quit your career because it is interfering with your "work-life balance" or because "the family is being neglected," they are unlikely to be able to enjoy your accomplishments and will even claim to be profoundly worried about it. Another strategy might be to pick a fight with you or have an emotional breakdown in the middle of an important work to make you uncomfortable.

Sign #5: They Only Have a Few Friends

Friendships are difficult for selfish people to maintain. It is possible that due to your love and devotion to your partner, you could be willing to overlook their ongoing selfishness. You constantly hope that your relationship will last because you see that they have the potential to become a more giving person in the future. Typically, relationships don't work out like that and you should take this sign to reconsider your future with your partner.

Sign #6: They are the Masters of Excuses

When someone constantly comes up with various excuses, it often indicates a self-centered attitude. This happens because, well, you know, some folks tend to focus on what they want and need first, kind of putting themselves ahead of others. They sometimes find ways to explain things away so they don't have to take responsibility or really put in genuine effort in their relationships or situations. It's like they're really into looking out for number one, without really considering how other folks might be feeling or what they might need. And because of this, their interactions with others can get pretty frustrating and shaky, you know, since this kind of behavior can mess with trust and all that.

Sign #7: They are Incredibly Defensive

Every time you question or confront them, they always respond defensively and will somehow try to blame you. They will take every possible step to hide their defects, even if it means drawing attention to yours. They won't ever admit wrongdoing and will look for opportunities to make you feel bad. They will not take criticism well as they believe that they are perfect. Their actions are cruel and unkind, and they believe that this behavior is totally acceptable.

Sign #8: They have Very Little Empathy for Others

Self-centered people believe that their problems are the only ones that matter and that the world revolves around them. They see your suffering or issues from their perspective and the way it affects them. They went through harder trials than you do. Self-centered people are unwilling to comprehend or understand the suffering of others. Since they think that the world, as well as you, exists for their advantage and wants, they have little consideration for how their actions may affect others.

Sign #9: Not Being Polite to You

When your significant other acts are impolite towards you, it might suggest that they're quite self-absorbed. It's like they're more wrapped up in their own desires and concerns, hardly thinking about how their actions or words might impact others. In a good, solid relationship, both partners treat each other kindly and respectfully, showing they truly treasure and look out for each other's happiness. A lack of civility could indicate that one is placing their own sentiments above that of their spouse.

Sign #10: They don't Try and Fix Things That Bother You

If you tell your partner that anything bothers you, they should try to resolve the issue so as to avoid getting worse but your feelings won't matter to a selfish person, and they'll continue to hurt you.

It can be challenging to see our partner's selfishness at times. Especially if we've grown in love with them, it's challenging. So now It may be the time to consider what you actually want if you realize that you are or may be dating a selfish person.

Future Planning:
9 Red Flags of Evasiveness

We've definitely experienced those moments when we attempt to share our future plans with our partners but end up getting caught up in a tangle of uncertainty and ambiguity. It's clear to all of us that a strong and positive partnership relies on open communication, trust, and shared objectives. But what happens when one partner starts displaying signs of evasiveness? Let's explore some red flags that someone might be avoiding giving you a clear answer, and how to navigate these situations for a more productive outcome.

Red Flag # 1. Elusive Details

Have you ever asked your partner about their future plans and received responses that sound more like vague responses than concrete information? Statements like "I'm still figuring things out" or "I'll see where life takes me" could signal evasiveness. When individuals offer few specifics or avoid discussing their plans in detail, it might be time to be on the lookout for hidden agendas or hesitations. Encourage open communication by expressing your interest in their plans and goals. Gently prompt them to share more details about their thought process. This can help create a comfortable environment where they feel more inclined to open up.

Red Flag # 2. Inconsistencies in Discourse

Inconsistencies in what your partner says can be a clear red flag. If their narrative changes from one conversation to another, or they provide different explanations for the same question, there might be something beneath the surface. These inconsistencies could indicate discomfort with revealing their true intentions. Approach the situation with understanding. Instead of pointing out the contradictions directly, ask open-ended questions that allow them to explain their thought process. This can help foster a sense of trust and honesty.

Red Flag # 3. Repetitive "Nos"

You're discussing plans with your better half, and every question you ask seems to be met with a resounding "no." While hesitation is natural, if someone consistently shoots down ideas or refuses to consider alternatives, it might indicate an underlying reluctance to engage in productive planning. You should shift the conversation from a 'yes' or 'no' framework to a more exploratory one. Present options in a non-threatening manner and encourage them to share their reservations. This can create space for constructive dialogue.

Red Flag # 4. Unusually Calm Demeanor

While maintaining composure is important, an unusual display of calmness in response to discussions about the future could be a sign of evasion. If someone appears overly composed or detached when discussing their plans, they might be concealing their true emotions or intentions. Validate their feelings by expressing understanding and empathy. Make it clear that you're interested in their perspective and that their emotions are valid. This can encourage them to share their thoughts more openly.

Red Flag # 5. Changes in Tone and Cadence

Have you ever picked up on the way your partner talks about future plans? It's interesting how even a subtle shift in their approach can make you stop and think, right? It's all about that subtle change in tone and cadence. When someone's avoiding discussing your shared future, their words might become less enthusiastic and less certain. Instead of brushing it off, try initiating a relaxed conversation about your future goals. Keep the atmosphere light and allow them to share their thoughts without feeling pressured.

Red Flag # 6. Too Defensive

Defensiveness is the classic human response when someone feels cornered or uncomfortable. If your partner becomes overly defensive when the topic of future plans arises, it might be a sign that they're evading the subject. But hold on! Instead of confronting them head-on, create an environment of understanding. Express your curiosity about their feelings and perspectives, emphasizing that you're genuinely interested in knowing where they stand.

Red Flag # 7. Concealing with a Confident Facade

You bring up the idea of future planning, and suddenly your partner becomes oddly smug, almost like they're hiding something behind that confident grin. It's crucial not to jump to conclusions, as there might be reasons beyond mere evasion. Instead of jumping into accusations, try expressing your personal thoughts and emotions about the situation. This approach can create a space for a genuine sharing of perspectives, potentially inspiring them to reciprocate in kind.

Red Flag # 8. Stalling the Conversation

We've all been there – you're talking about your future dreams together, and your partner seems to continually stall the conversation with vague promises or sudden topic changes. We shouldn't jump to conclusions, but this might be an indication of evasion. Instead of jumping to get answers from them immediately, maybe think about revisiting the topic when both of you have a good amount of time to really dive into it. This not only takes off any sense of urgency but also shows that you're okay with waiting for the perfect time.

Red Flag # 9. Keeping Their Phone Locked and Distant

In this digital age, smartphones have become an integral part of our lives, and that includes relationships. If you notice your partner becoming increasingly guarded about their phone – keeping it locked and maintaining distance while using it – it might raise some eyebrows. Respecting each other's privacy is important, but transparency is equally vital in a healthy relationship. Instead of confronting your partner in an accusatory manner, initiate a conversation about your own habits and views on privacy. Express your feelings about maintaining trust and openness in the relationship. This can create a platform for them to share their perspective on the issue without feeling defensive.

Future planning is a complex landscape that requires honest and open communication. By recognizing these red flags of evasiveness and adopting strategies to navigate them, we can foster healthier conversations that lead to more productive planning outcomes. Remember, the key lies in creating an environment where individuals feel comfortable sharing their thoughts and concerns, ultimately paving the way for a clearer, more collaborative future.

Manipulative Love:
8 Warning Signs of Coercive Control

Feeling confused or guilty without a clear reason? Manipulation could be at play. Some individuals, especially those who enjoy playing mind games, are skilled at identifying your vulnerabilities. They exploit these areas for their benefit, creating an ongoing cycle. Recognizing manipulation within your own relationship can be tough, especially if it started subtly. This article highlights how to spot clear signs of emotional manipulation and coercive control and provides guidance on responding to it.

Sign #1: Manipulative Distortion (Gaslighting)

A manipulative technique known as gaslighting might lead you to doubt the truthfulness of the abuse you're experiencing in a relationship. It's a technique used by abusers to get their victims to question their own sanity or judgment. If your partner hurts you intentionally and you confront them afterward, they may be gaslighting you if they claim things like, "That never happened" or "Oh my goodness, you're crazy!" The reaction aims to both deny and raise doubts about whether the incident actually occurred.

Sign #3: Emotional Isolation

In a relationship, you might start sensing a thing called "isolation" seeping in. It's when one partner begins to set boundaries on the other's connections with others. You know, it's like they're creating this tiny protective shield around you, causing you to feel a bit cut off from the rest of the world. This can lead you to feel pretty lonely and like your world revolves only around your relationship.

It's pretty messed up though, because this isolation game is actually a sneaky form of messing with your mind, kind of like psychological trickery. It's all about one partner trying to have the upper hand and keep you under their thumb. They can make you more dependent on them for emotional support, approval, and companionship by limiting your social interactions. This may make you feel vulnerable and make it more difficult for you to see the unhealthy relationship dynamics and the controlling partner's negative behavior.

Sign #4: Overemphasis on Their Favors

A person who tends to play with your emotions might suggest taking on tasks they don't really want to do, making it seem like they're doing you kindness. But watch out, because when you happen to disagree with them, they might flip the scene and use those past favors against you. It's like agreeing to whip up dinner every evening, and then down the line, they'll bring it up and remark, "I go out of my way to cook for you, and this is the thanks I get." Additionally, they could treat you with expensive vacations or presents before bringing it up as a favor during a disagreement.

Sign #5: Passive-aggressive Behavior

When someone can't quite explain their real feelings, it can be really frustrating. It's like they're playing mind games in the relationship. Other times, they go silent and look at you without saying anything, making you confused. And then there's that sneaky way of talking that's not direct - like when they smile but seem angry and say things like "Oh, I'm fine" when they're not really fine, or reply with a sarcastic "Thanks a lot" when you give them advice. To put it simply, the person is feeling bad but they don't want to or can't say it clearly.

Sign #6: Undermining Through Negging

Some tricky people might use a tactic called 'negging' to distract you. This tactic is like a move used by some people who try to impress others. They use it on people who might not feel very confident about themselves. Surprisingly, this tactic could actually work in different situations where you want someone to like you. It's a bit sneaky – you act like you're giving a compliment but also slide in a little tease. For example, saying, "You look nice, even though you've been eating snacks," or "You'd be even cooler if you weren't always so serious." crazy, right?

Sign #7: Superficial Charm and Excessive Niceness

A charmer will use flattery to get intimate, influencing, and having power over you. They are nasty creatures; thus, they are naturally charming. They don't hesitate to harm others. A manipulator will simply and without hesitation employ filthy techniques to lure or persuade someone, but a normal person would never do so. Human behavior is studied by manipulators. They interact with people to learn about their wants and requirements. When they learn that, they make you a similar offer in an attempt to win your trust. You should consider what someone might want from you if they are extremely charming and seductive toward you.

Sign #8: Demanding Proof of Your Affection

Watch out for partners who regularly put your love to the test, maybe by beginning their sentences with "If you really loved me." People sometimes use phrases like, "If you genuinely cared about me, you'd handle the chores," or even, "If you truly loved me, you'd want us to be close right now." These words can tap into our sense of duty and maybe even make us feel a bit awkward, pushing us to do things that might not be entirely reasonable or within our comfort zone. Despite its seemingly innocuous nature, this constitutes a form of influence.

Though identifying other varieties of influence could pose a challenge, being cognizant of these tactics can aid you in safeguarding yourself and making informed choices regarding your relationship. Persisting in a relationship where manipulation methods are frequently employed could potentially have adverse effects on your mental and emotional well-being. Change is possible, but the other person must take the initiative. This is why it's so important to put yourself first and develop ways to create distinct boundaries.

Mismatched Life Goals:
9 Red Flags of Incompatible Futures

Am I compatible with my partner? Many people constantly wonder whether or not they will have a future with their partner. Early signs of incompatibility can give you the option to leave the relationship or improve the balance. The presence of signs of compatibility does not only mean that you share the same interests. It can also mean, among other things, having the same intimate energy, feeling protected, being able to handle differences, and understanding one another while under pressure.

Sign #1: Humor Styles Are Out of Sync

One of the first signs that you're incompatible is when you can't get the jokes that the other person makes. In any relationship, humor should be appreciated because no one would like to stay with someone who lacks humor and someone who doesn't get their jokes, either. This sign might also imply that you don't comprehend one another's ways of thinking. Couples from different age groups are more likely to experience this.

Sign #2: All Your Acquaintances Are Urging You to Move On

Undoubtedly, our friends and family don't always know what's best for us, but in circumstances like a love relationship, it is easy to sense the depth of a relationship from a distance by loved ones. Your perception is affected by a variety of emotions, anxieties, biases, etc.

So, like, if all those people from the outside are dropping hints that they're not really vibing with the whole relationship situation, it might be a good idea to just take a moment and think about why they might feel that way.

Sign #3: Divergent Levels of Intellectual Compatibility

One of the clear symptoms of an incompatible relationship is when one partner has a doctorate and the other is a dropout. Intellectual differences may be overlooked at first since the couple enjoys one other's company and other qualities. However, once the initial period of love, at first sight, has passed, both partners will be able to recognize how distinct their respective educational backgrounds make them. This is not a constant sign, though; it might change depending on the relationship.

Sign#4: Varied Attachment Approaches

Getting a good grasp on your attachment style is pretty crucial. It comes in handy when you're trying to connect with a partner who vibes with you. Some people totally dig being all cozy and soaking up that touchy-feely stuff. On the other hand, some people find it a little overwhelming and aren't fully comfortable with it. There's no need to hide your desire for physical intimacy if you start to feel a little uncomfortable or aren't in the mood for a cuddle sesh.

Sign#5: You both are stubborn.

When both people in a relationship are really set in their ways and don't budge, it can end up causing some serious compatibility issues. It's like, if neither person is willing to give a little or compromise, it can lead to a lot of friction and make things pretty tough between them. It's a matter of personalities clashing. People that are stubborn typically refuse to apologize or acknowledge their mistakes and will stand their ground regardless of the circumstances. Can you imagine what might happen in the event that two stubborn persons disagreed?

Sign #6: Clashing Perspectives on Financial Matters

Most of the decisions you two will make together are likely to be shaped by your financial situation. Making sure your finances are stable becomes crucial if you're planning to build a family or share a life under one roof. It's essential to come to a mutual understanding of your financial priorities to ensure your future objectives align. For instance, if one of you enjoys indulging in luxurious spending while the other prefers a more frugal approach, finding a middle ground might prove to be quite challenging. Keeping separate bank accounts might reduce the chance of arguments related to money.

Sign #7: Absence of Genuine Affection

When you see your lover, does your heart begin to race? Although it's likely that things used to be that way, feelings sometimes change or evolve through time. Don't you find it kind of intriguing how folks can end up sticking around in a relationship, even when they sort of sense that things might not be perfectly balanced on the emotional or intimate front? It's really important to engage in those deep, honest conversations and tackle any problems head-on once you start sensing that the special connection you used to share with your partner isn't quite as vibrant as it used to be. Taking this step can actually help keep the situation from escalating further.

Sign #8: Relief Sets in When Your Partner's Absent

Do you enjoy time spent with your partner? The answer to maybe one of the easiest questions will indicate whether or not your relationship is having problems. Do you generally find that you enjoy yourself more without them, even when you're just hanging out by yourself? Sometimes we receive feelings from our subconscious minds that we are only partially aware of. If you feel relaxed when your partner is not around, you most likely hold a deeper belief about the relationship that is the root of your unhappy feelings.

Sign #9: Conflicting Timetables

When partners have completely different schedules, it can really throw a wrench into a relationship, you know? Like, if one person's grinding from nine to five and the other's hustling' the night shift or whatnot, it's going to be a real challenge to sync up for chill sessions, convo, or shared activities. When you can't carve out that special time or have those deep talks, it's a real struggle to truly click and weave a solid connection.

Being in a relationship is based on the thought that you belong together. It's not that you won't have disagreements and heartbreak; nonetheless, incompatibility makes things difficult. However, if you and the other person are on the same page, you can tackle minor issues. I hope these 9 signs help you identify the underlying cause of tension in your relationship.

Red Flags of Neglect:
8 Signs of Unresponsive Partner

Relationships can be like delicate flowers that need nurturing and care to bloom beautifully. Relationships are built stronger when you get undivided attention from your partner. But what happens if you begin to notice minute changes in your relationship with the person you love? It's time to pay attention to those red flags of neglect. In this section, we're diving into the signs that your partner might be becoming unresponsive and distant.

Red Flag # 1. Neglecting The Importance of Quality Time Together

Remember those cozy movie nights, long walks in the park, and those endless conversations that used to make your heart skip a beat? If these moments are becoming scarce, it's a definite red flag. Lack of quality time together can signal that your partner might be withdrawing emotionally. Instead of just ignoring, open up a dialogue with your partner about how you're feeling. Share your desire to spend more quality time together, and brainstorm activities you both enjoy. By setting aside dedicated time for each other, you can rekindle the flame and strengthen your bond.

Red Flag # 2. Little to No Significance of Physical Affection

From holding hands to those warm embraces, physical affection is a powerful way of expressing love. So, if you've noticed a decrease in cuddles, kisses, and hugs, it's time to take notice. Reduced physical affection might indicate emotional distance. You should Initiate small acts of physical affection yourself. A simple touch or a loving gesture can send a message of closeness. Additionally, engage in open conversations about your need for physical intimacy and learn about your partner's perspective as well.

Red Flag # 3. Unbalanced Focus in the Relationship

Relationships work best when both partners contribute to the fulfillment and expansion of the union. It's an indication of imbalance if you see that your partner's wants are constantly prioritized, while your own worries are put on the back burner. Communication is key! Have an honest conversation about your feelings and the dynamics in the relationship. Express your desire for mutual support and active participation in each other's lives. Finding ways to share responsibilities and decision-making can bring back a sense of equality.

Red Flag # 4. Not Being Confident Enough to Share News

Remember when you looked forward to telling all your exciting stories to your partner? Well, it's a really big warning sign right there if you've kind of realized that you're not really that person they're eager to share with anymore, or they're not as curious about what's going on with you. Make an effort to ensure that you two can communicate honestly and openly. Encourage each other to share daily experiences, thoughts, and feelings. By actively listening and showing genuine interest, you can rebuild a sense of connection and emotional intimacy.

Red Flag # 5. Feeling Taken for Granted

Have you ever experienced a situation when you put up a lot of effort and go above and beyond, but it seems your efforts are going unnoticed? Like, even if you're there, giving it your all, and attempting to make things work, it's possible that your spouse isn't totally supportive of everything you're working on. It would be beneficial to take a moment to reflect on your future steps. You know, relationships thrive on this balance of sharing and taking and showing that two-way street of respect. Express how you're feeling without blaming them. Honest conversations can work wonders in bringing back the balance. Share how their actions make you feel and encourage them to share their perspective too.

Red Flag # 6. The Silent Treatment

The silent treatment – it's like being stuck in a maze with no way out. When your partner goes all quiet whenever there's a problem at hand, it's a pretty clear indicator that something might be off. You know, communication is like the bedrock of any good relationship, and clamming up just doesn't really do any favors. Instead of trying to crack some kind of mysterious code, it's usually a good move to just have a heartfelt chat and let your partner know you're there to chat whenever they're up for it. Initiate a calm conversation about the silent treatment. Let them know that open communication is essential for resolving conflicts. Express your willingness to listen and understand their point of view.

Red Flag # 7. Unclear Expectations

Ever felt like you're navigating a minefield of expectations with no map in hand? Building strong relationships often thrives on honest communication. So why not take a short break, engage in a pleasant conversation, and share your ideas on your goals, objectives, and passions? Start a casual conversation about your hopes and encourage your partner to do the same. Just make sure it's a comfy zone where you both can spill your thoughts without worrying about someone pointing fingers.

Red Flag # 8. Uncomfortable Around Loved Ones

Your partner should be your safe haven, right? If you notice that you're suddenly uncomfortable around your own friends and family when your partner is present, that's a cause for concern. Healthy relationships should foster an environment of support and acceptance. Let them know about your feeling of discomfort that just won't go away. Ask them to be supportive in every situation and be kind towards you as they are your partner and this is your right to ask them to completely understand what is bothering you and what is not.

Every relationship has its good times and challenging times, but catching these signals early can seriously change the game. So, if any of these warning signs hit close to home, take action. Relationships are totally worth the energy, and by dealing with these issues, you're moving closer to a more satisfying and bonded partnership. Stay tuned for more heartfelt discussions about love, life, and everything in between!

Blatant Disrespect:
Recognizing 9 Red Flags of Disregard

Respect is the foundation of every strong relationship, a relation in which both people respect each other's feelings and needs, they are both willing to calmly discuss issues and at times ready to make acceptable compromises. Unfortunately, rude behavior is also common in relationships. It's important to understand the signs of disrespect and how to respond to your partner who doesn't treat you well because it might have serious consequences.

We'll concentrate on some of the warning signs of relationships in this section

Sign #1: No care for your safety

Have you ever felt unsafe while being around your partner? This situation could potentially indicate a lack of regard within a relationship. To illustrate, if you find yourself thinking that your significant other might compromise your safety while driving—whether it's by speeding excessively, getting too engrossed in other things, or failing to focus on the road—it suggests that they may not be valuing not only your emotions but also your well-being.

Sign #2: They Don't Listen When You're Talking

A big signal of disrespect is when your significant other brushes off your words or outright ignores them. It really makes you wonder – if they can't even put in the effort to pay attention, how much do they truly value you and your thoughts?

Now, it's natural to let it slide once in a while, but if this becomes a recurring theme, it's a clear indication that your partner might not hold you in high regard. I mean, if they genuinely respected you, they would definitely treasure and acknowledge the thoughts you bring to the table.

Sign #3: Acting Bossy

Is your significant other all about keeping tabs on what you're up to? Do they seem to have this urge to oversee every little detail in the relationship? Are they always dictating exactly how you should go about things, to the extent that it's taking a toll on your peace of mind? If so, your partner is bossy and in power. This is a serious disrespectful problem in a relationship. They do not respect your thoughts when they talk over you, insult your accomplishments, or make decisions on your behalf, which are all examples of microaggressions and disrespect. This might lead to tension and dissatisfaction in your relationship as you may frequently engage in power battles with your partner.

Sign #4: Not Apologizing

Even happy marriages experience arguments and problems. However, the success of the relationship depends on how the couple resolves their differences and deals with the issue. Regardless of who is at blame, the couple must possess the humility to apologize and at times lift the white flag.

However, if you find yourself making excuses all the time while your lover takes pleasure in it, something isn't right. The incapacity of your partner to accept responsibility shows that they don't respect your ideas and feelings. The hardest mistakes to overlook are infidelity and mental and physical abuse. These actions are typically not tolerated, and sometimes even apologies are useless. But it's always preferable to accept blame and apologize for minor mistakes that they make.

Sign #5: They push your physical boundaries, even in "innocent" ways

When you ask your partner to stop tickling you, do they continue to do so? When you ask for personal space, do they continue touching you in seemingly normal ways like hugs, shoulder rubs, or even continuously poking you in the arm like a sibling? Just like in any relationship, it's important to ensure that the guidelines we establish for others are treated with respect. The matter at hand here is about how things can escalate. When a significant other crosses the line when it comes to your personal boundaries, it might suggest that this lack of respect could persist over time. It's crucial that individuals can comprehend and give due consideration to simple yet powerful words like "no" and "stop."

Sign #6: Hot and cold behavior

When a partner is "hot and cold," it usually indicates they have a pattern of acting badly or hurting your feelings, followed by a lot of apologizing. In order to win you back again, the apology will typically take the shape of romantic gestures like flowers and presents and a promise to never do it again.

You know, it's interesting how we often hold onto hope that things will get better in a relationship. But the tricky part is, we tend to focus on the good moments and conveniently let go of the not-so-great ones. Breaking free from this pattern can be a real challenge, so it's pretty crucial to catch yourself doing it and acknowledge it early on.

Sign #7: They Don't Bother to Keep Promises.

Breaking commitments in a love relationship is a huge sign of disrespect. To show your efforts and validate the marriage and your partner, it is of the utmost importance to be faithful to your ward. It should always be a priority for you to keep your word to your partner.

Sign #8: They Make Decisions Without You.

If your partner doesn't respect you, they won't bother asking your opinion before making important choices in your relationship. They disregard your role in their relationship and act in their best interests, whether it's making a big purchase or choosing a career. Selfish and disrespectful behavior is demonstrated by this.

Sign #9: Difficulty sharing feelings.

Intimacy begins with the sharing of our feelings. It is a significant red flag if either one of you, or both of you, are unable to recognize and express your emotions in a healthy manner in your communication and intimate relationships.

When you notice red flags early in a relationship, take note of them. You should take the situation seriously and assess how it might affect your relationship moving ahead, whether you are encountering lies, dealing with possessiveness, or being put down.

Social Media Clues:
Recognizing 9 Red Flags of Privacy Disregard

People can now date and find partners much more easily, thanks to social media. Couples who live far apart and in different time zones can now stay in touch. Despite these advantages, social media may also play a role in breakups. It's now simpler than ever to catch your significant other in the act when they're up to no good because it is a public platform. For instance, In the comments, you can find them making flirtatious comments to random people or notice that they were tagged in a recent picture with their ex.

Following are some red flags that could be a real cause of a breakup.

Sign #1: Relationship Status = Single

You should never feel hidden in your relationship. Pure-hearted people do not keep their lovers a secret. When someone hides something, they are trying to keep it a secret from others. This normally indicates that someone has an affair with someone else or It might also imply that someone important in their life does not approve of them seeing you. It's a problem even though it's not cheating. A person ought to defend the relationship they choose.

Another possibility is that your partner is ashamed to be dating you. They openly reject you, which actually presents more issues than cheating. This requires counseling to continue growing together in the relationship. People who are dishonest often give up stories that they prefer to keep their private lives private.

Sign #2: Not tagging you in photos

It is natural for your partner to tag you in photos they share or post when you are in a committed relationship. It may be difficult to determine whether they value you and your relationship with them if they are intentionally ignoring you and failing to tag you in any pictures. It is assumed that something is wrong if they neglect you or treat your presence on social media like it doesn't exist.

Sign #3: They have multiple secret accounts

On social media platforms, some users have several accounts because they use them for various purposes, such as having private and professional profiles, but having many secret accounts is entirely different. This typically indicates that they have something to hide, and if your significant other is doing so, it is a matter of concern.

Sign #4: Not sharing details of their social media accounts

People in relationships might be hesitant about sharing their social media details because they value privacy and control. They might use their online presence to manipulate or deceive their partner, and sharing details could expose their hidden actions. By keeping their details private, they can continue their manipulative behavior without their partner knowing, which helps them maintain power and control over the relationship. It's important to understand that strong relationships are built on mutual respect, trust, and honesty; withholding social media details for manipulative purposes runs contrary to these values.

Sign #5: They post flirty comments

You should be suspicious of your partner's intentions if they feel the need to leave a flirtatious comment or suggestive emoji on another person's photo, especially someone they don't know very well. Commenting that their friend looks good isn't a problem at all, it's always nice to compliment people. However, making inappropriate comments about their exes or other unknowns raises a big red flag.

Sign #6: They Constantly Seek Attention Online

While you love looking at their selfies, there are moments when it seems like they post too much about themselves. They post selfies of themselves doing the most monotonous activities, posing for photos, and modeling in almost the same pose repeatedly. With all the albums of selfies they've posted, it might soon get awkward. This could be a deceitful tactic to attract attention. They may be looking for external validation from others, which is a warning sign.

Sign #7: Stalking their ex

Stalking an ex online is one of the major relationship red flags. Alarm bells need to go on in your head if your partner spends their leisure time snooping through their ex's social media. This typically indicates that they haven't really moved on from them whereas someone who's healed and moved on will be focused on your life together and moving forward.

Sign #8: Hidden Messages

Now people can delete messages or put their messenger in a mode that hides their chat on the majority of social networking platforms. You should be concerned if your partner acts in this way. They are probably cheating or engaged in suspicious activities if you notice them deleting texts or using private messaging mode. You can figure out if your partner hides communications without snooping. You might observe someone physically delete a message or notice that their message screen is darker. It's a red flag when they are constantly uncomfortable around you and they always open their phone and turn the screen away from you.

Sign #9: They're comparing your relationship to what they see online

Insecure couples are obsessed with presenting a certain image online. This is a highly embellished and curated selection of moments from their lives which has nothing to do with reality. Unfortunately, those who are dissatisfied with their own life may believe these fantasies to be true. This isn't right if your partner makes comparisons between your relationship and delusional relationships that they see on social media.

Recognizing red signs is one thing, but taking action on them can feel challenging, particularly if you've built anger or irritation. It's crucial to prioritize your own health first. Social media red flags can be quite frustrating, even though they're not always as bad as they initially seem. In the end, we all know that social media can be toxic.

Red Flags of Flirting with Others:
Signs of Potential Cheating

Being cheated on and lied to is the worst feeling ever and it can shatter your trust into pieces. However, you believe it or not, there are always signs before something like this happens in a relationship but we deliberately decide to turn a blind eye to these clear red flags so that we can deny the reality that is looking us right in the eyes.

If you also feel like your partner is either lying to you or flirting with other people behind your back, then here are a few signs that you should look out for in your partner. In this section, we will point out some of the telltale signs that your partner is flirting with other people.

Sign#1: They are Overprotective of their Electronic Devices

If your partner gets uncomfortable whenever you try to use their phone, it's a huge red flag. Only those people who are hiding something are overprotective of their Electronic Devices. If their mobile is always locked and they keep it face down whenever they are in the same room with you, it's a visible sign that they are trying to hide their mobile notifications from you.

Having a password on your phone and mobile is common, however, if they never let you use their electronic devices, even in the time of an emergency, it is a sign that your partner might be flirting with other people online or having a secret affair. In situations like these, it is important to follow your gut feeling and confront your partner in a healthy manner.

Sign#2: They Complain About You

Complaining that you no longer look attractive or can't fulfill their needs emotionally and sexually is another sign that your partner is probably not happy in their relationship and they are communicating it in a very unhealthy and toxic way. They may also compare you to other people and their partners to make you feel like you are not trying hard enough to be your best version.

The constant comparing and critiquing can make you feel like you can never be good enough no matter how hard you try. Keep in mind that these complaints don't need to be always out in the open, subtle constant complaints are also a red flag. If your partner is trying to flirt with other people, he or she may also complain about you to his friends and colleagues or among a group of people.

Sign #3: Projection and Insecurity

One of the biggest red flags is projecting things and being insecure. Cheaters, when confronted about it, often start projecting it on you. They feel targeted and when they cannot think of any good explanation, they will blame you for cheating and neglecting them. This will make you feel guilty hence changing the trajectory of your conversation.

For instance, if you ask your partner about something that you have been finding suspicious and they start inquiring about someone else and starts accusing you of cheating, then that probably means that they are hiding something and using an unhealthy defense mechanism to cover their lies. Another sign of cheating and flirting with others is insecurity, your partner will openly flirt with other people, however, when you do the same thing, they will be extremely insecure and jealous. They will try to make you feel guilty while doing the same thing. This is one of the biggest signs that your partner is flirting with other people to stroke his ego. However, when you try to give him the state of his own medicine, he gets extremely defensive and insecure.

Sign#4: They Disappear

Being stood up is unacceptable and it points out that your partner is either involved with someone else or is no longer attracted to you. If they make plans and cancel on you at the very last minute, then it's a clear sign that they don't want to spend time with you. Or perhaps, they always have an important meeting or a work thing going on whenever you say you want to go out or spend time together.

They might tell you that they are busy and they have a lot going on, but you should always keep one thing in mind: if they want, they will. Spending time with your partner is important to have a healthy and trusting relationship, and if he or she is not ready to do that, then this could mean that they are spending their free time somewhere else

Sign# 5: Checking out other people

Whether in real life or on Instagram, if your partner is checking out other people, it's considered cheating. It is an evident red flag, especially when they are doing it right in front of your eyes. You might see their eyes drifting away from your face to someone else passing by in a restaurant or a mall, and this feels devastating.

When confronted about it, they will say that it was nothing and that you are being crazy. They will also try to normalize it and make you feel like you are the impulsive and obsessive one in the relationship.

Sign 6: Complimenting other people

Sometimes, it happens right in front of your eyes and you can't tell if they are really flirting or it's a figment of your imagination. When your partner is trying to flirt with someone at a party right in front of your eyes, they will give them an unnecessary and unnatural amount of compliments. They will try to compare you to them and make you feel insecure.

At the end of the day, there are always signs! Cheating and infidelity don't happen overnight, it takes a lot of ignored red flags. It's time that you recognize these red flags. And if you think that your partner is doing all of these things, then before jumping to any conclusion, you should healthily confront them so that both of you could move forward from this -alone or together.

Apology Red Flags:
5 Signs for Differentiating Sincere from Manipulative

As human beings, we are far from perfect. Be it our work, academics, or relationships —we mess up all the time. And it is only natural for us to make mistakes. Because if we won't make mistakes, we could never learn and grow. Saying something wrong and hurting your partner unintentionally doesn't make you a bad person, but you should know how to mend things and apologize.

It takes great vulnerability to accept your mistake and apologize for it. However, an apology could be sincere and heartfelt or it could be empty and manipulative. And we are sure that all of us have received an empty apology before.

Being forgiving is a great trait, especially in a relationship. However, sometimes you have to open your eyes to the truth and recognize whether their apology is sincere or not. To make it easier for you, we have put together 5 telling signs of a fake apology!

Sign#1: They are apologizing only to end the argument

It goes without saying that when you apologize only to end a conversation, it is a huge red flag. Some people cannot endure confrontation, and instead of communicating their feelings, they'd rather apologize and walk away from the situation. While in their heart, they still feel like they were not in the wrong. They will assume that they are being the bigger person by apologizing and ending the argument.

Not only is this form of apology manipulative and fake but it is also counterproductive. Ending an argument without communicating and talking it through will leave it unresolved. And one thing that you should always keep in mind is that unresolved arguments always come back. And no one would spend another two hours bickering about the same thing again and again. So if your partner is apologizing and you know that they are only doing it for the sake of ending the argument, then you should encourage them to be honest and communicate what they are actually feeling even if it is not what you want to hear.

Sign#2: Their apology is more about them

The biggest sign of a manipulative apology is that it is always followed by a hundred reasons and excuses. It is more about what they are feeling and justifying their wrongdoings than pacifying the one who is being wronged. Always remember that a sincere apology is supposed to empathize with the victim, not a mere excuse for what the perpetrator has done.

A fake apology will always seek sympathy and ways to make you guilty about being hurt in the first place. They will present reasons to portray themselves as victims, and the next minute, you will be the one apologizing. You should be able to recognize that this is a red flag and apologies like these are nothing but toxic and manipulative.

Sign#3: Their apology doesn't change anything

Yes, your partner apologizes every time. They won't let you be mad for too long and always accept their mistake, but do they change?

Do they try to fix the mistake and make sure that it doesn't happen again? And if your answer is a no, then all their apologies are meaningless. The mere purpose of an apology is to realize your mistake and ensure that it won't happen again, otherwise, what's the point of apologizing in the first place?

If you complain about something, it is their responsibility –if they agree with it –to fix their mistake. Only apologizing is not gonna do anything, you have to reflect it into your actions. Always bear in mind that actions speak louder than words. Their apology could be a poetic masterpiece but they are only empty words if you see no change in their actions.

Sign#4: Their apology doesn't take any responsibility for their actions

What does a fake apology sound like? When they are apologizing but you see them not taking any responsibility for what they have done. For instance, instead of saying, *"I am sorry I made you feel this way"*, they say, *"I am sorry you feel this way"*

What they are doing here is acknowledging what you are feeling and empathizing with you, but they are not taking any responsibility for it. In simple words, they don't think it is their fault that you are feeling this way and they believe that their actions had nothing to do with it. This kind of apology might make you feel heard and understood, but in reality, you are being blamed for being hurt.

If your partner expresses that he or she is hurt, you should always apologize for making them feel this way even if it is not what you intended to do. Even if they are misunderstanding you and being irrational, you should always apologize and later explain that you didn't want them to feel this way.

Sign#5: Their apology always has a 'but' attached to it

An apology that is always followed by a "but" is a red flag. What happens is their apology becomes a part of their sentence, rather than being a sentence in itself. If you are sincere, your apology should end then and there. I am sorry. The end. Period.

"I am sorry but..."

This sentence always ends in projecting and blaming the other one. If their apology is always followed by a 'but', then it is not an apology. End of the story. They are apologizing just to get your sympathy and to tell you that they are the real victims here and they are hurting more than you.

At the end of the day, you should never jump to conclusions and label someone toxic or a red flag immediately after hearing a fake apology. It is important to understand that not everyone understands these things and having control over your emotions is the best way to deal with hurtful situations. Explain to them why you think their apology is fake and manipulative. Give them logical reasons for feeling this way and communicate with each other to move past this.

Gaslighting Signs:
Recognizing Red Flags of Manipulation

Gaslighting is a term that has been thrown a lot on the internet lately. So much so that it has been declared Word of the Year by Merriam-Webster. So what does Gaslighting mean? Merriam-Webster defines Gaslighting as an "act of intently and grossly misleading someone – especially for your own advantage"

Gaslighting is the biggest red flag in a relationship and it means that your partner is manipulating you to the point where you start questioning your own reality. Gaslighting leaves you feeling insecure and unsure about your decisions and actions. It erodes your self-confidence.

The beauty of being gaslit is that you don't even realize that it's happening to you –at least not until you are pushed to a deep end. It's essential to realize the red flags of emotional manipulation in a relationship at the right time. Here are a few solid red flags in a relationship that will help you recognize a Gaslighter.

Sign#1: They Deny Objective Facts

The biggest sign that your partner is Gaslighting you is that they keep denying things that are right in front of you. For instance, if you are telling a story and it is not playing out the way they want, they will interrupt you and say *"That never happened"*

When you confront them about something, they will completely deny the fact, "I never gave her my phone number". Their lies will be confident and direct. They won't hesitate a second before calling you a liar. For them, you will always be the delusional one who is making up things on their own. They will constantly accuse you of making things up when you are telling the truth. When you are upset, they will make you feel like you are overthinking and being crazy.

Sign#2: They will criticize you subtly

People who gaslight want to make their partners feel insecure. They do this to gain a sense of control and power in relationships. To do this, they insult you subtly. They point out things about you to people and to you that are not true. *"Of course, you misplaced the keys! You are the most careless and unorganized person I have ever seen"*

Comments like these make you believe that you are in fact whatever they say you are. They also mention things like these to people they know, *"How can she ever manage without me? She is so forgetful and keeps misplacing things"*

This will slowly eat away your pride and self-confidence. You will start thinking that you can never be good enough and this is extremely detrimental to your mental health and stability.

Sign#3: They accuse you of doing things that they are doing

Projecting their mistakes on you is another red flag in a relationship. People who take advantage of their partner's nice and people-pleasing side always look for ways to make them feel guilty. Whenever they are confronted about something, they will either plainly deny it or start projecting it on you. If you ask them, "Who is this in your messages, are you cheating on me?" They will say, "You talk to your friends all the time. I don't even know what you do all day. Maybe *you* are cheating on me"

Insinuating their mistakes on you is an easy way out for them. This way, they will get you to explain instead of answering for their actions.

Sign#4: They insult people and things close to you

Another sign of a Gaslighter is that they will always make you feel bad about things you like and people who are dear to you. They will constantly insult your family and make fun of your hobbies. They do this to feel good about themselves and keep you off-balance.

Sign#5: Their actions are inconsistent with their words

When you are being Gaslighted, you start believing things that are not actually happening. If your partner is Gaslighting you, he or she will say something else and do the opposite. For instance, they will keep projecting how much they help you and take care of you, while in reality, they are doing none of those things.

Sign#6: They lie about what people say about you

One of the biggest red flags that you are being manipulated in a relationship is if they lie to you about what other people think about you —especially those close to you. They will tell you how someone said something bad about you to make you lose trust in that person. These people don't want you to trust anyone so they can keep manipulating you and using it for their own advantage.

By doing this, they are not only making you lose trust in people close to you, but they are also making you think that whatever these people are saying about you is true.

Sign#7: They use your friends against you

Another sign of being emotionally abused in a relationship is that your partner is slowly turning your friends against you. He or she constantly complains about you to people who are close to you. He criticizes you in front of other people and masks it with concern, eventually turning people against you.

Sign#8: They call you paranoid

When you can no longer tell the difference between what's real and what's not, they call you hysterical and paranoid. They will do things to hurt you, and when you tell them how bad you feel, they will deny everything and call you crazy.

If you can relate to all of these red flags, then you are being emotionally manipulated. It is extremely dangerous for your mental and physical health to stay with a person like this. We know that it can be hard to speak up and make a choice to get out of an emotionally abusive relationship, but it is the right call. If you are feeling like you are being gaslit in a relationship, then you should seek help from people around you. Talk about it with your friends and observe the patterns they are using to emotionally manipulate you.

Ignoring Intuition:
Why Dismissing Gut Feeling is a Red Flag

Going against your gut feeling is self-deception. You are only trying to deny what is right in front of you. While sometimes it may seem unethical and wrong to follow your gut feeling, the best decision you can make is to listen to what your mind and body is telling you. However, you should never do it blindly.

This leaves us with a burning question: when should you follow your gut feeling and when should you ignore it?

Well, there are a few circumstances when trusting your gut is your best option. Especially in a relationship, it's better to be certain now than regret forever. Here are eight reasons why dismissing your gut feeling in certain situations can be a red flag

Sign#1: You should trust your experience

If a series of decisions lead you somewhere wrong, your mind is very likely to remember it. Over time and with experience, you develop a feeling that we call 'gut feeling'. This intuition is mostly based on our bad experiences and failures, and when it tells you something, you should listen.

If you always feel uneasy, nervous, and worried around your partner that you will trip a wrong switch, then it is a red flag that you shouldn't avoid. A healthy relationship allows you to be yourself and introduce your partner to your friends and family without any hesitation. If you don't experience this ease and comfort with your partner, then you need to listen to your gut feeling. Always remember that a relationship that starts badly is very unlikely to improve with time and hard work.

Sign#2: Asking questions leads to the truth

Whenever there is infidelity involved, there are always signs. It doesn't happen out of nowhere, there is a trail of ignored red flags and signs that leads to a complete picture. While it is unethical to snoop around someone's phone, you should look for opportunities to ask your partner for his passkey. If they are hesitant and won't let you open their phone, then it is a huge sign that something is cooking behind your back.

Ask questions. Keep an eye. Investigate. Whenever you get together with your friends, try to observe and listen to the things they are talking about. When they are late, ask where they have been. Keep in touch with their colleagues so that they can't lie about overtime. If you feel like your partner is cheating on you, you should always ask. However, if their explanation seems empty and unsatisfactory, trust your gut. Do what you think is necessary to find out the truth. It is better than being cheated on and turning a blind eye

Sign#3: Trust your emotions

Always remember: even a wrong clock is right twice a day.

If you are feeling ill at ease, worried, skeptical, or insecure, more times than not, then it means something. No one is irrational, paranoid, and crazy all the time. We use these excuses to push negative thoughts away from our minds and play make-belief that our relationship is sustainable. Instead of living a delusional life, you should trust your emotions and confront your partner. If they habitually dismiss or try to turn the tables by blaming you, then this is a clear indicator that this relationship might not be sustainable.

Sign#4: You should be able to rely on your partner

We all know that there are days when everything is just spiraling out of control. But these days only happen once in a blue moon. If your partner hangs up on you, shows up late, or simply doesn't show up at all, then this indicates they are lying to you about being busy.

One thing that you should always remember about human nature is that we do whatever we want to do. So if he wanted to come home on time, he would have. And especially if it keeps happening again and again and you are left to pick up the crumbs of affection after him, then you should question the very nature of your relationship.

Sign#5: Follow your instincts

How many times in your life have you suspected a hunch and talked yourself out of it? Only to find out later that your instincts were right. This is called ignoring your intuition and it is never good. Your instincts have been established based on your failures, feelings, and past experiences. They teach you something very valuable: they teach you how to survive.

You might tell yourself, "No, I am just being paranoid". And it might be true but if the feeling doesn't go away even after talking to your partner, there is something wrong. Some people keep ignoring it and even marry the wrong person until they have no choice but to face the bitter truth.

Sign#6: Acknowledge your insecurity

Most of the time, your insecurities are deeply related to how your partner treats you and what their level of commitment is to you. If you feel insecure about your relationship, it is important to communicate this to your partner.

Sign#7: Look for a pattern

Try to use logical reasoning when you feel anxious about your relationship. Observe their behavior and try to understand why they might be behaving peculiarly. And most importantly, communicate. This will help you in realizing a pattern. And if it's repetitive and obvious then it might be the right time for you to pull the reins.

Sign#8: They dodge your questions

To follow your gut feeling, you will have to ask questions and make sure that it is not what you think it is. If your partner constantly dismisses you and dodges your questions, then your gut feeling is probably right.

Trusting your gut feeling is always a good thing. For starters, it is designed to protect you. Moreover, it allows you to build trust. You can only trust people if you follow your instincts and make sure that they are not lying to you.

Red Flags of Hidden Relationship:
Signs of Secrecy

Distrust in a relationship is a plaque that slowly erodes your bond, memories, and time together. Not only being cheated on is extremely hurtful, but it also completely shatters your self-worth and confidence.

If you doubt that your partner is seeing someone else, then you should always look for signs of secrecy. Is he hiding something from you? Does he no longer trust you with his phone? He isn't as attracted to you as he used to be? Does he disappear without telling you? If you nodded to all of these questions, then there is a chance that your partner is involved with someone else behind your back.

Whether you agree with us or not —a cheater always leaves a trail of signs and red flags behind. It is you who decide to ignore them in the hope of being swept away with love. If you have a feeling that your partner is hiding something for you, then look for these signs. In this section, we will tell you eight telltale signs that your partner is hiding a secret affair.

Sign#1: Disappearing without any explanation

How many times have you been excited about a plan only for him to cancel on you at the last minute? Does he bail on you without explaining where he is going? He often returns home late and sometimes doesn't show up at all. These are all red flags.

Long unexplained disappearances can only mean one thing: he is spending his free time somewhere else or with someone else. Canceling on you last minute and never asking you out are all signs that he doesn't want to spend time with you. If you feel like you are being neglected in a relationship, it is important to communicate it with your partner.

Sign#2: Hiding phone and electronic devices

Another sign that your partner might be having a secret affair is him being extremely secretive and protective about his phone and electronic devices. Think about it, if he has a girlfriend, he will naturally communicate with her through his phone. Being overly protective of their phone is a red flag that indicates he has something in his phone that he doesn't want you to see.

Sign#3: Lying

If you have been noticing that your partner has started to lie to you over small things, then it's a sign. Behind small and insignificant lies, there is always a bigger reason. As they say, tell a lie and the rest come easily. If your partner is cheating on you, he or she will go to lengths to keep that thing hidden. For that, they will have to lie –a lot!

They will lie about where they have been, why they are late, and who they are talking to. The lies become evident very quickly. You just have to keep your eyes open. If you decide to keep your eyes shut on purpose, there is no one who can help you.

Sign#4: Projecting

Another thing about liars is that they get defensive when you confront them about their lies. If your partner is hiding something from you and you confront them about it, chances are they will either completely deny it or start projecting it on you. This is called Gaslighting. They will make you feel guilty for even doubting them in the first place.

Instead of explaining their lie, they will start accusing you of doing something that they have been doing. Projecting their mistakes on you is a great way for them to make you feel like you are at fault. So if you decide to ask your partner about a lie he has told and he tries to turn the tables by accusing you, then it probably means that he is hiding something and trying to pin it on you.

Sign#5: Neglecting and avoiding you

Have you ever wondered why your partner doesn't ever invite you to his office parties and friends' dinners? Why have you never even met some of his close friends and their girlfriends? The answer to this is simple, he doesn't want you to know what he does when you are not around.

There are things that his friends know about him that he wants to hide from you. Perhaps a secret fling, a one-night stand, or hitting on a girl in a mart?

Another red flag is that he avoids you. He doesn't like to talk to you more than necessary. This is their guilty conscience. They can't look you in the eye and talk to you like everything is okay because they know that they are nothing but pathological liars.

Sign#6: Spending money on someone else

If your partner is having a secret affair, he will start spending an excessive amount of money. Spending money and not explaining it is a big red flag. It means there is someone who he is buying gifts and going out with.

Sign#7: Having multiple social media accounts

If your partner is cheating on you with someone else, chances are they are communicating with that person using a second Instagram account. If he doesn't want the other girl to know that he is committed, this is an obvious option. Besides, only those people who have something to hide have secret social media accounts. So if they have an account that you are not aware of, then this is a sign that he is trying to hide something from you.

Sign#8: Attending mysterious work calls

If you have ever seen your partner talking in hushed tones in the middle of the night, then it is a little suspicious. Getting consistent work calls, which he attends to well out of your earshot is a sign that something is not right.

At the end of the day, you can't rely on these signs to decide whether your partner is hiding something from you or not. If you doubt his intentions, you should communicate your fears and suspicions to your partner and see how he reacts to them.

Signs of Dismissive Behavior:
6 Red Flags in Communication

The key to a healthy relationship is healthy communication. Poor communication is always responsible for leading your relationship to estrangement. Lack of emotional intimacy makes you feel like you are talking to a brick wall. Conversations between you and your partner are usually heated and counterproductive. Both of you have lowered your level of understanding and you don't even recognize the person sitting in front of you. All of these are signs of poor communication and dismissive behavior

Humans are dynamic beings and we need to constantly learn about each other. If we stop doing this, we will lose our place in people's lives and vice versa. Initially, you might have some valid reasons for poor communication like wariness or work-related stress. However, it's important to understand your partner's needs too. In this section, we will tell you six signs of bad communication in a relationship so that you can improve and learn to understand each other

Sign#1: Using Generalized Language

Be it you or your partner, using generalized language to explain someone's action leads to unhealthy and passive-aggressive communication. How would you feel if your partner uses a single instance to describe your entire personality? Horrible, right?

Statements like *"you always do…."* and *"You never understand…"* are all red flags in communication. Using these sentences in an argument means that you are ignoring everything good your partner has ever done. Using generalized language is only going to steer your conversation toward a conflict. Therefore, you should have a healthy conversation and convey this to your partner

Sign#2: Ending Argument Quickly

Another red flag is wanting to end the argument without truly resolving it. Sure, no one likes to fight. However, you should always talk things out and let them go completely before moving on. If you are apologizing just for the sake of ending an argument, this is not a healthy sign. Unresolved conflicts and arguments always come back.

You should always listen to each other and understand where the other person is coming from. This is the only way you can resolve an argument and move ahead. On the other hand, if you won't talk it out, there will be unsaid things left behind which is a sign of poor communication.

Sign#3: Making Assumptions

Using statements like, *"You must not like me anymore…."* or *"I bet you can't even stand me…"* is another sign that your communication is faltering. Making assumptions about your partner's feelings is not allowing both of you to grow and understand each other. This will only put your partner's feelings in a box and cause a huge communication gap.

Even if you are feeling these things, there is a healthier and better way to put it out there. You are always allowed to express your feelings –how you do it matters a lot. You can talk to your partner and tell them you have been feeling like they are drawing away or are not attracted to you anymore. This way both of you will be able to communicate and understand each other without relying on baseless assumptions.

Sign#4: Silent Treatment

Most people, when they are hurt or angry, decide to go into a silent mood. While it is important to understand your partner's coping techniques, talking is also important. If you will ignore your and your partner's feelings after an argument it is only going to make things worse.

If you or your partner goes silent after a conflict, it is important to give them time and space. However, not talking about it for long might make the other person feel like they are being abandoned and neglected. It is important that you communicate in some way that you are taking your time and that you are not ignoring them. Assure your partner that you will be ready to talk once you are feeling better.

Sign#5: Arguing over events based on subjective truth

You should always understand that there are many parts to a story. Couples often fight over events based on subjective versions of the same story of the past. We are all different human beings and we have different perspectives. It is normal if you recount a memory differently and your partner remembers it in a completely different way. Arguing over it is completely baseless and counterproductive. You cannot change someone else's perspective or version of the truth.

If you find yourself in a situation like this, you should always try to find a middle ground instead of fighting over events based on subjective truths. You can communicate this by saying *"You must have seen and interpreted it differently, but to me it was like this….."*

This is a healthy way to understand each other's version of the story and get a third perspective on it.

Sign#6: Not recognizing each other's input

Relationships only work if both partners are putting something on the table and it is very important to recognize each other's input. If you don't want to listen and recognize the other person's effort, then nothing can save your relationship. Not being able to recognize good in your partner is a huge red flag. If you can't see anything good in them, then what is the point of dating that person?

Lack of communication is not something you can't work on. However, you should always be open to self-scrutiny. Realize what are some unhealthy things that you need to change in yourself. It always starts with improving yourself. Listen to each other and say what's on your mind too. For good communication, you need to do both simultaneously –listen and express.

Talk to your partner about your feelings without playing the blame game. Avoid generalized statements and try to find a middle ground. Letting things go unresolved is a huge sign of poor communication. Always try to talk and express what you are feeling. Similarly, let your partner talk and when he talks, do not only listen but try to truly understand where he is coming from.

www.ingramcontent.com/pod-product-compliance
Lightning Source LLC
Chambersburg PA
CBHW071450080526
44587CB00014B/2054